PATHBREAKER PARENTING

NEW CONVERSATIONS TO ENGAGE YOUR TEEN AND EMPOWER SELF-DIRECTED THRIVING

SETH MARLOWE

SPARK Publications
Charlotte, North Carolina

PATHBREAKER PARENTING
New Conversations to Engage Your Teen and Empower Self-Directed Thriving
Seth Marlowe

Designed, produced, and published by SPARK Publications
SPARKpublications.com
Charlotte, North Carolina

Icons by Lauren Marlowe
Photo Illustration by solarseven / shutterstock.com and SPARK Publications

Printed in the United States of America

Paperback, May 2024, ISBN: 978-1-953555-69-4
Library of Congress Control Number: 2024909093

Dedication

Donna: without my rock by my side, nothing would be possible. We wrote this book together during the many hours spent discussing what we might do next to help our two knuckleheads find their way in life. I hope the pages of this book reflect the depth of my love and appreciation for all that you are and serve as a tribute to the countless ways you've enriched my life and the lives of our daughters.

Lauren and Brooke, you each became a purpose the day you were born, and seeing you thrive is the greatest joy any parent could wish for. I hope the pages of this book serve as a testament to the love and lessons we've shared and spark empowering conversations between parents and teens everywhere.

Table of Contents

SECTION 3 THE PATH

SECTION 4 GROWTH MINDSET

SECTION 5 THRIVE

Prologue

My wife and I raised two daughters, now twenty-three and twenty-six years old. Like you (I hope), we love our daughters endlessly and want to help each of them become thriving (a keyword you'll see a lot in this book) young adults who achieve happiness and fulfillment throughout their lives. And, like you, we were relentlessly pressured to indoctrinate them to a one-size-fits-all path during their teenage years.

My wife and I said "nope" and raised them to ignore much of what the adults in their lives will insist they prioritize, decide, commit to, and complete. We didn't do a few things differently here and there; we did most everything differently, through an interwoven series of conversations I share in this book. Even though they are diametrically different humans, each is now a thriving, self-confident, financially independent, and pleasant young adult.

While this book is not a parent brag, context matters. According to the rules in our society, these now-thriving young women were destined for failure: two terrifically unremarkable teenagers on their way to Loserville, population them. Our oldest daughter was even called into the principal's office in high school for a one-on-one lecture about how she was "wasting her potential" by proactively deciding she did not need to go to college (and never wavering).

They both attended school because it's the law and stuff. But neither achieved a single accolade or academic recognition award. Neither played a sport for or in any way represented their school. Neither campaigned for, much less were elected as, class president or anything similar. Neither was the "It" girl, ran in the popular crowd, or was chosen as most likely to be anything in their senior yearbook. Neither spent a semester abroad, held an internship, or wasted time contemplating what they wanted to "be." Neither developed what anyone would consider to be a strong work ethic (a total of two part-time jobs in high school). Neither attended a private school or expensive tutoring sessions.

Zero money or time was spent preparing for the SAT (one of them never took it). One never applied to a college; the other applied, was accepted, went for one semester, and dropped out. At twenty-two, when these young women were supposed to have demonstrated proof of academic excellence, perseverance, and obedience by holding a piece of paper that made them eligible for financial success and happiness, neither displayed the slightest bit of conformity.

And it was all by design.

"The most educated (and in debt) generation in history is pouring their heart, mind, mental wellness, and a lot of money into a formulaic path that, for many, does not work out as expected."

SECTION 1

HOUSTON, WE HAVE A PROBLEM

It's never been more apparent that the academic-laden, task-heavy, spend-whatever-it-takes approach to raising kids in our society is unnecessary at best and disastrous at worst.

Teenagers are increasingly stressed out and anxious and view their futures with such fear and despair that many must be medicated to get through their day. Not surprisingly, these teenagers often become timid and unhappy young adults struggling to find the fulfillment and financial success they were promised. And many enter the real world with crushing debt that acts as a two-ton boat anchor on their hopes and dreams.

This isn't an opinion; it's the reality in our society. But it doesn't have to be the reality for your teenager.

CHAPTER 1

Young Adults Struggle

As a parent, what is the goal? Most of us say the goal is to enable our children to become thriving young adults with a strong foundation that leads to prolonged and, mostly, happy lives. Once our children venture out independently, we hope they secure full-time work, financially support themselves, build healthy relationships, and make (mostly) good decisions while being strong-minded enough to manage their way through life's ups and downs. So, how are we doing? Not very well.

Compared to their peers from forty years ago, far fewer twenty-one-year-olds (Figure 1) reach any life milestone—especially financial ones. By age twenty-five (Figure 2), today's young adults still lag behind on financial milestones; many live with their parents and are far less likely to be married or have children.

There are, of course, many circumstances and beliefs regarding such data. For example, some may not believe in the institution of marriage. Additionally, people can thrive while living with their parents, and only some want to have children. Nitpick if you must, but don't miss the forest for the trees. Young adults are struggling—big time—to financially provide for their needs (housing, food, transportation, travel, etc.), build healthy relationships, and self-direct their happiness.

Figure 1.
Studies like this one show today's twenty-one-year-olds significantly trail their peers from forty years ago.

At age 21, today's young adults lag behind earlier young adults on major life milestones

% of 21-year-olds in the United States who have completed each milestone

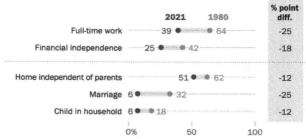

Note: Financial independence refers to having an income of at least 150% of the poverty level for one person in a given year. Marriage refers to being currently or ever married.
Source: Pew Research Center analysis of 1980 decennial census and 2021 American Community Survey (IPUMS).

PEW RESEARCH CENTER

Figure 2.
The same study shows today's twenty-five-year-olds are increasingly delayed in achieving life milestones.

Today's 25-year-olds are nearly on par with earlier young adults on key financial milestones

% of 25-year-olds in the United States who have completed each milestone

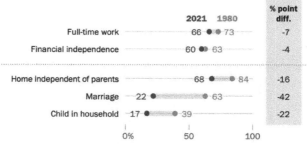

Note: Financial independence refers to having an income of at least 150% of the poverty level for one person in a given year. Marriage refers to being currently or ever married.
Source: Pew Research Center analysis of 1980 decennial census and 2021 American Community Survey (IPUMS).

PEW RESEARCH CENTER

(Source: Richard Fry, "Young Adults in the U.S. Are Reaching Key Life Milestones Later than in the Past," *Pew Research Center*, May 23, 2023.)

Not surprisingly, these struggles lead to frustration and unhappiness. While data and research are compelling, what most convinced me are open and honest conversations with young adults. I ask them about their current reality, what was emphasized as a teenager, and how they're doing today. I repeatedly hear four themes during these conversations.

1. My hard-won college degree is not magically opening doors.
2. The pressure to choose a career without real-world experience leaves me feeling trapped.
3. Hard work and dedication aren't leading to the success and moneymaking I anticipated.
4. I constantly chase and fail to meet the expectations I brought with me into the real world.

Not every young adult shares these themes, and some are perfectly content with where they are in life. But, again, there is more than enough evidence that what we're doing is not working—especially when one considers the massive investments being made to prevent this problem.

Why are young people so miserable?

They tally lowest life-satisfaction scores among all age groups of those 18 and older in Harvard-led study, reversal of results of past surveys

BY Alvin Powell
Harvard Staff Writer

SHARE ✉ f 𝕐 in

DATE September 15, 2022

Figure 3. This article states that the degree to which young adults are unhappy is "pretty striking, pretty disturbing."

(Source: Alvin Powell, "Why Are Young People So Miserable?," *The Harvard Gazette*, September 15, 2022.)

The most educated (and in debt) generation in history is pouring its heart, mind, mental wellness, and a *lot* of money into a formulaic path that, for many, does not work out as expected. Young adults often feel disillusioned and frustrated because they were misled, only to be called entitled by those who misled them.

CHAPTER 2

A Misguided Path

While theories abound about the cause of this problem and why it continues to worsen, I believe much of it relates to how teenagers are raised and what they're led to believe. The adults in their lives—from parents to coaches to guidance counselors to family members and beyond—indoctrinate teenagers to the critical importance of a "path" that must be followed, no matter the costs.

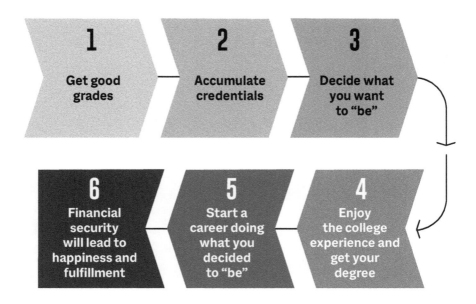

At its core, the path centers on avoiding uncertainty by presenting the illusion of known outcomes. Teenagers, constantly inundated with media signals about how volatile and dangerous the world is, find comfort in a "Just do what you're told, and it will all be okay" mentality and are indoctrinated into a worth-it-at-all-costs, step-by-step path.

You'll be all set if you follow the rules, do what you're told, complete the assignments, and accumulate the required credentials. Even better, the path includes a handy-dandy grading system that means you know how you're doing and what you're capable of. If you make As, you're smart and will be successful. If you make Bs or Cs, either you're not reaching your potential and need to shape up or just accept that you can only achieve limited success. If you make Ds or—God forbid—Fs, you will likely be a loser who lives paycheck to paycheck.

What could be better than a simple, rules-based system in which you always know where you stand and how much potential you possess? What could be better than an input-output-based system in which the more effort, time, focus, and money you invest, the more successful you will be when you exit it? What could be wrong with that, everyone asks?

What's wrong is that teenagers—constantly goaded on by the adults in their lives—maniacally focus on completing assignments, taking tests, chasing grades, stockpiling achievements, and hoping to be accepted by a "good" college. Suppose they ever stop to question it all and ask why they're relentlessly forced to comply and perform. In that case, they're reminded it's all for their own good. "We just want you to be happy," they're told.

Time, stress, anxiety, money, worry, and effort are all *required* because college is more than a fantastic experience where you forge lifelong friendships, establish a network, and have fun. Upon graduating, you possess the credential that unlocks eligibility to attain your potential and, most importantly, financial success. With the credential, the world is your oyster, and without the credential, you'll always be limited. And how do you not just attain but *maximize* your potential and financial success? Simple. The more prestigious the college that bestows your degree, the more unlimited your potential and financial success.

If we're being honest with ourselves, that is the snake oil we're selling to kids, right?

Teenagers aren't mentored and guided to explore, experiment, and conduct activities that cause them to feel innately accomplished and fulfilled. They aren't encouraged to be a kid, have fun, and gradually decipher what lights them up on the inside. They aren't empowered to self-direct their learning, expectations, and mindset. They aren't inspired to experience what things cost, dabble in value creation, and construct a lifestyle they choose. There is no time for that nonsense!

They must focus on getting into a "good" college because maximizing their potential and making lots of money will lead to happiness. Said differently, compliance in the present will result in happiness in the future.

With that directive in mind and lacking a solid case to dissuade the jury, they pour their time and energy into checking boxes, hanging out with friends, and desperately seeking distractions. And that leaves no time, much less guidance, to develop one core and critically important capability. They exit the path and enter the real world with little to no ability to *self-direct their happiness and fulfillment from the inside out.*

And, for most of them, that dormant volcano eventually erupts.

CHAPTER 3

The Requirement Lie

Teenagers are relentlessly implored to follow and excel on the path based on a known and unquestioned fact: a college degree is *the* key that unlocks unlimited earning potential and higher job satisfaction throughout their career because the best jobs and promotions *require* a college degree. And even if the requirement were to become less prominent, the college experience and induction into the "degree club" is too compelling to ignore. It's what successful people do.

The college industry is damn good at marketing their snake oil; it all makes for a compelling argument, and almost everyone takes the bait. Except here's the thing:

It's a lie.

College can be a wonderful experience with lifelong friendships, knowledge attainment, and other benefits. No doubt. But, as you'll learn in Section 3 of this book, the insistence that the best jobs and promotions require a college degree is a lie. How do I know this? Two reasons.

First, Figure 4 is a screenshot of the actual job description for the role our oldest daughter, Lauren (now twenty-six), was promoted to in 2022 at a Fortune 200 company. Despite never spending a minute in a college classroom, much less possessing a college degree, she is now six years into a high-paying career and landed a role she was repeatedly told, as a teenager, would be inaccessible without a

Required

- Bachelor's degree in a relevant field preferred (Human-Computer Interaction, information design, communications, Computer Systems, etc.)
- 3+ years of experience in UI/UX design
- Proficiency using UX and protyping tools (Axure, Sketch, Adobe Creative Cloud, InVision, etc.)
- Experience with WCAG accessibility standards
- Proven effectiveness in working as a member in cross-functional teams which include business analysts, designers, researchers, developers, and product owners
- Experience with Agile and/or lean philosophy and methods
- Design experience for both web and mobile
- Ability to create wireframes as well as visual design comps
- Portfolio examples of sketches, workflows, interactions, and end state work
- Up-to-date with the latest UI trends, techniques, and technologies
- A user-centered approach in design perspective and practice
- Excellent verbal and written communication skills
- Positive attitude and be able to work effectively in a team
- Strong sense of accountability and drive to get results
- High attention to detail but able to work quickly to meet deadlines
- Ability to solve problems creatively and effectively
- Maintain a user-centered approach in design perspective and practice
- Must be legally authorized to work in the United States for any employer without sponsorship
- Successful completion of interview required to meet job qualification
- Reliable, punctual attendance is an essential function of the position

Preferred

- lAirline experience
- Preferred CISSP, CISA, or CISM
- Understanding of HTML, JavaScript & CSS

Figure 4. An example of the typical job description used to convince teenagers that a college degree is required for "good" jobs.

college degree. As I'll explain later, she didn't even take the SAT because she knew at sixteen that she would skip college and never wavered throughout high school.

I know what you're probably thinking: "A bachelor's degree is listed right there in writing as the first required item. If she didn't go to college, did she lie about her credentials, circumvent the process, or misrepresent herself?" Nope, none of that was necessary.

As I'll explain in this book and walk through step-by-step in the final section, Lauren was taught at a young age to ignore what people tell her is supposedly required to land a good job or be promoted because most human beings do not refer to credentials when they make decisions about who they value. She was also taught that requirements like a college degree and years of experience are mostly filtering mechanisms used in online application systems (I'll explain later). As a result, she started her career as a UX/UI Designer at twenty, landed her dream job at twenty-three, and is consistently told she will have no limitations in her career. She loves her job, has zero debt, and earns more than the average Harvard graduate at the same age.

Second, I know the statement that a college degree is necessary is a lie because we spent time online entering search phrases such as "How to become a _____ without a college degree" and discussing the results.

How to Become a Financial Advisor Without a Degree

Jun 16, 2022 — **Working as a financial advisor does not require a college degree,** although most people working as financial advisors do have four-year degrees.

How To Get Into Marketing Without a Degree [Career Guide]

Aug 31, 2022 — Can You Become a Marketer Without a Degree? ... Yes. Many experts in the field didn't have marketing degrees when they got their first job, and ...

How To Become An Interior Designer Without A Degree?

So, to answer the question, **yes, indeed, it is possible to become an** interior designer without getting a degree in design. It is more about having the required ...

10 Sales Jobs You Can Land Without a Degree in 2023

Sep 8, 2022 — **No, you don't need a degree to work in sales.** You can get into sales without a college degree, though it does help to have completed a relevant ...

Figure 5. You and your teenager can learn how to enter almost any career without a college degree via an online search.

Sit down with your teenager and enter anything you want—engineer, nurse, accountant, interior designer, marketer, salesperson, business owner, financial adviser—and you'll find what we found. Are there certain jobs that, by law, require specific certifications? Absolutely, and I will cover that, but make no mistake, a college degree is rarely required to land almost any job.

While some people will concur and agree that it might be possible to land a job without a college degree, their position hardens when it comes to maximizing potential and financial success. "Sure, you might be able to land a job," they say, "but what about promotions and reaching the highest levels of a corporation? What if you want to be a senior executive or company CEO? *That* is why a college degree is critical. It removes all ceilings."

We'll go deep into this topic later, but let's quickly address that position by returning to Lauren's journey (so far). Now, six years, four roles, and two promotions into a career she was repeatedly told in high school would require a college degree, she's never felt the need to hide anything or hope no one noticed the missing required credentials on her resume. And never, not once, has anyone presented this as an issue or problem in an interview or evaluation because—drumroll please—*nobody* cares.

Why? Just think about it from a personal perspective.

If you rely on someone to do meaningful work and she consistently delivers beyond what's expected, has a great attitude, and gets things done—would you value her? Would you find yourself looking for ways to keep her around? Would you give her formidable problems to solve?

Yeah, me too.

Suppose you pondered how she acquired her technical skills, developed a stellar attitude, and learned the importance of creating value for others. Would you care that she didn't follow the conventional path? Would you place a ceiling on her if you discovered she chose not to go to college and, instead, self-directed her learning?

Yeah, me neither.

Would you even be impressed that she became so valuable by *not* doing what everybody else did? Would you want to know how she did it? Would you hope her self-confidence and originality rubbed off on her coworkers?

Yeah, me too.

It's how we all operate. You likely celebrate those who do things you assume couldn't be done. You wish you could be the maverick who thumbs their nose at conformity; you cheer for the underdog and love to see the little guy stick it to the big guy. But then, you stop daydreaming and return to insisting your teenager comply.

Finish their homework. Complete another college application. Study extra hard for their biology test. All the while convincing yourself it's for their own good.

You're the parent, and your job is to ensure your child does what's required because you couldn't live with yourself if they were to be released into adulthood without the option to maximize their potential. With that in mind, perhaps reluctantly, you become a taskmaster. You poke, prod, cajole, prompt, and remind. When you fail to get through, and an important task or assignment isn't complete, you swoop in to complete it. If they're at risk of getting a bad grade on a project or significant exam, you beg them to focus. If necessary and/or possible, you do the work for them. All because they don't know any better, but you do.

Here's the thing, though. Instead of mentoring and guiding your teen to flourish across all life domains, embracing confident self-direction and priming them for a thriving future, you are pushing all your chips to the center of the table based on a playbook that became obsolete at least two decades ago.

It's time to make a change.

CHAPTER 4

Start New Conversations

This book unleashes you from an obsolete and irrelevant role. Your task-mastering days will soon be a thing of the past as you start new conversations that foster a shift in parental roles, empowering you to become an enabler while allowing your teen the autonomy to navigate as a self-directed individual.

Your new conversations have one thing in common with the old ones.

The Path	New Conversations
Be a kind, responsible, helpful, respected, contributing member of society	Be a kind, responsible, helpful, respected, contributing member of society

Otherwise, everything will be different.

The Path	New Conversations
Learning is done to you	Learning is something you choose to do
Financial success leads to happiness and fulfillment	Happiness and fulfillment lead to success
Fixed mindset: Present as smart (i.e., grades) and don't risk being perceived as otherwise	Growth mindset: Don't present as anything; try stuff, be curious, fail often
Fear uncertainty and seek formulaic outcomes	Embrace uncertainty and excel at zigging
Life can be a plan with steps to execute	Life is a roller coaster; throw your hands up
Invest and commit based on averages	Averages do not apply to individuals
Completing tasks assigned by others is a valued skill	Task proficiency is table stakes; be a linchpin
Conformity is a sought-after character trait	Conformity is boring; make a ruckus
Mistakes go on your "permanent record"	Make mistakes as often as possible
Your potential has a ceiling	Your potential increases daily
Risk is dangerous and unsafe	Risk is doing things without known results
Credentials prove you're persistent and hardworking	Most credentials are lazy filtering mechanisms
What do you want to be?	What do you want to try first?

These conversations are not about coddling your teenager, bending to their will, or letting them do whatever they want. Instead, these conversations establish a new mindset, release pressure, and create space for ongoing and constructive dialogue. You and your teenager will adopt a growth mindset, prioritize new behaviors and goals, and invest time, energy, and money differently. I encourage you to put this book down and start your first conversation right now (then pick it back up; we've got work to do!).

From this point forward, we will pivot and take a new approach to your development.

- *You will not be pressured to follow a one-size-fits-all path because you're a unique individual capable of designing (with our help) your journey.*
- *You will not be forced to learn things against your will because you will be too busy developing the ability to confidently self-direct your learning.*
- *You will complete tasks assigned by others when necessary, but your priority will be proficiency at setting and achieving your own tasks.*
- *You will not believe you must become eligible for financial security. You will, instead, establish and learn to fund your desired lifestyle while everyone else chases eligibility.*
- *You will not expect happiness and fulfillment to be a by-product of financial success. You will take the opposite approach.*
- *You will not blindly assume college is the best option after high school. You will energetically explore all the options.*
- *You will not waste time stressing over what you want to "be" because doing so is a pointless exercise. You will, instead, focus on what you want to try first.*

We will embark on this journey together and enable each other along the way. But, make no mistake, this new approach puts you in the driver's seat with me/us riding shotgun. You will be newly empowered as we focus on two core goals.

First, you will build foundational and transferable traits and skills that make you universally invaluable and always in high demand. Second, and most importantly, you will learn how to self-direct your happiness from the inside out and become empowered to achieve your interpretation of success, no one else's.

I can't wait to get started.

These conversations are *not* for people who crave safety and a formulaic "Just tell me what to do, and I'll do it" approach. Some people are convinced the path is the best way to succeed and be happy. Some people believe the upside of college is priceless, no matter the individual. I get it, but this approach is not for those people.

These conversations are *not* for the rule follower who struggles with swimming upstream while everyone in their social circle floats downstream. If fitting in is your jam, this ain't for you. Trust me. You will be overwhelmed by the criticism and judgment that come with thumbing your nose at the path's most zealous followers and champions.

And, last, these conversations are *not* for the parent who lacks the time or desire to be a true mentor. If you expect or need the "system" to dictate how your teenager invests their time and energy, with you in a taskmaster role, this is a waste of your time.

These conversations *are* for someone who knows that being safe and formulaic is overrated at best and soul crushing at worst. You don't want your teenager to grow up avoiding risk and playing it safe; you want your teenager to become a fierce, confident, self-motivated badass.

These conversations *are* for someone with the emotional intelligence and self-confidence to stare down those zealous path followers and say, "Hold my beer." They will come at you like a spider monkey (*Talladega Nights* reference there; I hope it landed), but you will stay calm, avoid direct eye contact, and refrain from feeding them.

These conversations *are* for someone ready to dedicate their time and energy very differently. While your friends and peers will fret over homework, test scores, and flawless college applications, you and your teenager will bond over insightful, enriching, and stimulating interactions as you plant, water, and fertilize seeds.

And, last, these conversations *are* for someone not seduced by a quick fix. This approach is meant for the parent of a twelve(ish) to sixteen(ish)-year-old with hundreds of days and tens of thousands of hours to work with. You are not rushed, beholden to fictional deadlines, or the least bit apprehensive about uncertainty. Instead, you're cementing an indestructible foundation and helping your teenager build the floors of a burgeoning skyscraper.

I break it all down into four sections after this one. In Section 2, I share eleven short anecdotes that drove my belief system and conviction. In Section 3, I walk through and dismantle the path step-by-step because it's essential to understand what's being done to your teenager. In Section 4, I help you build the right mindset in yourself and your teenager to enable new conversations and a new journey. In Section 5, I provide the details on what conversations to start holding and how to best invest your and your teenager's time, energy, and resources in a far more impactful way.

Without further ado, let's get into it.

"I learned life is entirely unpredictable. Thinking you can plan everything out is fruitless. But, on the flip side, my daughter taught me one thing with complete and final certainty: mindset is *everything*."

SECTION 2

WHAT DROVE MY CONVICTION

You must reach a strong point of conviction to write a book. It didn't happen overnight for me; instead, it was a slow drip over the years until I told my wife, "I think I'm going to start that book everyone tells me I should write." Like anyone, countless events, decisions, mistakes, and situations formed my belief system. As I looked back, these eleven experiences are why you're holding this book in your hand.

Maybe you can relate to a few of them.

CHAPTER 5

School

MIDDLE-CLASS KID IN A PRIVATE SCHOOL

I grew up in a middle-class household. Dad was a branch manager for a regional bank, and Mom was a high school math teacher. While Dad dropped out of college after two years, education was paramount to Mom because she viewed her master's degree as the critical achievement that enabled her to rise from poverty. She grew up in a three-room house with four siblings in a small town in Georgia.

Before I started second grade, Mom got a job at a new and prestigious private school. One of the perks was that if you worked at the school, your kids attended for free. From second grade through high school graduation, I received a "top-notch" education while interacting with rich kids who I assumed had the inside track to success and happiness.

What drove my conviction: As a middle-class kid attending a school with kids who lived in large houses, drove nice cars, and sometimes had a pool in their backyard I noticed things. According to the word commonly used today, these kids were "privileged," but many were unhappy, lonely, and anxious. And I caught glimpses of the tremendous pressure to meet or exceed the expectations of wealthy parents. Those moments left the lasting impression that pursuing money can have potentially damaging ripple effects.

MASTER'S DEGREE WITH NO DIRECTION

Despite being constantly prodded to try harder and commit to my schoolwork, I was disinterested. As a result, I did not get picked by my desired "good" college (University of North Carolina at Chapel Hill) and set off to attend the only other college I applied to (Appalachian State University).

Mediocre performance at a high-end private school enabled me to get a partial academic scholarship that I subsequently lost after one semester. Mom and Dad were unhappy and demanded more effort. Still, I remained unremarkable and never achieved a high enough GPA to get the scholarship back. I was apathetic about schoolwork and did the minimum to get by.

I decided to major in business halfway through college because why not? I had yet to decide what to do as I approached graduation and was too lazy to put much effort into figuring it out. I opted to stay and get my MBA, specializing in finance and taking out $6,000 in student loans. While my decision to pursue an MBA made my parents (especially Mom) proud, I mostly did it because I didn't want to be an adult.

School just never did it for me. I rarely engaged with or felt like I enjoyed what I was supposedly learning. Throughout high school and college, I found that most (not all) of us thought the same way. As I got older and listened to how teenagers describe how they felt about school, their words were the same as mine, one generation earlier.

What drove my conviction: After eleven years at a prestigious private school and five years of college, I exited the education system with an MBA degree that was supposed to put me ahead. Those sixteen years, however, did nothing to clarify what I wanted to do during the forty-plus hours each week I was now expected to earn income. Two questions entered and stayed in my mind: What and who was I ahead of? And why do we strongly emphasize excellence within a system most participants dislike?

CREATE A JOB FROM THIN AIR

Once I couldn't postpone adulthood any further, I had to get a job. I interviewed with a few financial services companies, but I was going through the motions. Less than two months before completing my MBA, I had no job offer and decided, "Dude, you need to do something here." If you graduated from college and had just about any amount of potential, moving back in with your parents was highly frowned upon at that time.

In grad school, one of my classes required me to be a student consultant for a small manufacturing company about forty-five minutes from campus. My assignment was to evaluate their business and present recommendations at the end of the semester. My primary recommendation was to invest in an enterprise resource planning (ERP) system, and the CEO expressed excitement about the ROI I told him he could expect (I had no idea what I was saying). Remembering that reaction, I decided to call and ask if they had followed through on the recommendation. They had not yet, and an idea popped into my head.

I wrote a one-page job description to own the process of evaluating, selecting, and implementing a new ERP system. I added miscellaneous IT tasks I had no clue how to do and some "financial analyst" value I thought I could deliver (and never did). Finally, I recapped the ROI and asked for a higher salary than that offered by other entry-level jobs I had interviewed for with financial services companies.

I called back, got an appointment, made the forty-five-minute drive, sat in front of the CEO, and pitched my job description. Thirty minutes later, he said, "Let's do it." I drove back to campus with my first job locked up, and the entire process took about five hours of work over three days.

I palpably remember being proud of myself.

What drove my conviction: Although I didn't know it then, the mindset I present in this book was sparked during those three days. You can do what everyone else does (interview for jobs in your "field" and hope to be picked) *or* create your job from thin air.

CHAPTER 6

Career

FIRED WITHIN FOUR MONTHS

Several months after starting my job, the ERP project went nowhere. I tried to deliver value, learned a good bit about IT work (spent zero time in college on that), and attempted to assist people on the finance team who (correctly so) wanted nothing to do with my "textbook" advice.

One Thursday afternoon, the new COO (hired two weeks earlier by the CEO) walked into my office and fired me. He told me I wasn't worth what I was being paid, and they didn't know when, or even if, the ERP project would start. He sent me home for the day and told me, "Come back tomorrow to gather your things and hand off your work to others." I was devastated.

The following day, I showed up and immediately encountered a weird vibe. About fifteen minutes after I arrived, the CEO walked into my office and said, "Forget what you heard yesterday. I want you to stay, and we will kick off the ERP project soon." Say what?

A couple of hours after I left the previous day, the new COO had sexually harassed our Office Manager and was fired on the spot.

What drove my conviction: This experience was a huge wake-up call. Despite the CEO's initial commitment to the project I proposed and led, I had made no progress after several months. I would have been unemployed with twenty-four hours' notice if not for a regrettable circumstance. I learned that attending a prestigious private school, securing an MBA, and getting hired by a company's CEO ensures nothing.

There is no such thing as "my job." No one is obligated to employ or promote me. No one is compelled to follow through on what is committed to me, and my entire world can be turned upside down at a moment's notice. I learned this lesson again, in the worst way possible, twenty-three years later.

ONE COLD CALL CHANGES EVERYTHING

A few weeks later, I was reviewing ERP vendor brochures (Google didn't exist yet) and got a cold call from a salesperson. He didn't know we were searching for a new system; the company I worked for was on his "call list" that day. A little over a year later, the ERP product he represented was live at our company, and we had become good friends (still are).

One day, he asked, "You're personable and know our software front to back—would you want to work for our company in a sales role?"

"Of course not," I said. "I've got an MBA in finance, and my next job needs to be in that field because that's what I'm qualified to do. Plus, I don't know the first thing about selling."

We had several conversations, and a key mentor convinced me it was a good opportunity and, potentially, a great career path. Three months later, I was in a sales role at a software company, and I (happily) remain in that field today.

What drove my conviction: There were two essential elements. First, within my first few weeks doing a job for which I had zero formal training, I quickly realized I could learn to do something while being paid to do it. I vividly remember thinking, "I'm starting to get pretty good at this, even though I didn't learn any of it in college." Why had it always been ingrained in me that the *one* right approach was to pay to learn something before doing it?

Second, once again, was the randomness of life. Even today, I often think back to how a cold call led to a purchase, which led to a friendship, which led to an opportunity, which ultimately led to a long and successful career. I never saw it coming when I took that call. You never do.

CHAPTER 7

Parenting

LEARNING TO RIDE A BIKE

One of my favorite memories of our youngest daughter, Brooke, is of the day she learned to ride a bike. My wife and I still love watching a video I recorded a few moments after she "got it."

One day, a few years later, we watched the video and a thought entered my mind. Did Brooke want to learn how to ride a bike because we told her to? Of course not.

Maybe she saw other kids riding a bike, which looked fun, or she thought it would provide a new sense of freedom. Whatever the

Figure 6. Our youngest daughter, Brooke, jumping with glee the day she learned to ride a bike.

reasons, she decided to learn how to ride a bike and was determined to do it. She started very unsure of herself. She was scared, fell a few times, became frustrated, doubted herself, and cried. But, after each fall, she was willing to try again to achieve the "reward" of her desired outcome. She was, literally, willing to bleed. And then, once she got it, she was so proud of her accomplishment and rode that bike for hours on end.

What drove my conviction: It hit me then—no one needs to "learn how to learn." Ever since that day, I roll my eyes (on the inside, I'm not a monster) when people say that. At school, learning was being done to my daughters. No more. I decided that learning will be something they choose to do because if you're determined to learn something, you'll do whatever it takes. Sometimes, you'll be willing to bleed.

THE WORLD IS FLAT

In 2006, almost ten years into being a parent, I read the book *The World Is Flat* by Thomas Friedman. This was approximately ten years after the internet became a thing. I was rocking a BlackBerry because the iPhone was a year from its iconic launch. It was also about twelve years after the NAFTA agreement was signed.

Friedman opened my eyes to the simultaneous explosion of the internet and globalization. The world wasn't slowly evolving with tweaks in the margins—the world was *rapidly* changing with massive shifts everywhere you looked. I took away three conclusions that caused me to rethink how we would raise our daughters and what we would prioritize in their teen years.

First, access to information was exploding. Anyone will be able to learn anything from anywhere. Second, as a business and an individual, you would compete globally, not locally. Differentiate or die. Third, for centuries at a time, things stayed the same, and playing it safe had many advantages. No more. Change would be the new world order.

What drove my conviction: Although our daughters were just six and nine at the time, *The World Is Flat* convinced me to start paying attention to the rapidly changing world and consider how it would impact them as they grew up. I became convinced that, by the time my daughters reached young adulthood, the traditional approach—going to school, getting a job, working that same job for decades, and retiring—would no longer apply. I wasn't quite sure what to do, but my antenna was raised.

LAZY SATURDAY MORNING

Eight years later, I found clarity on a lazy Saturday morning in the fall of 2014. I came across an e-book called *Stop Stealing Dreams* by Seth Godin that focused on one question. What is school for?

I had never asked myself that question (have you?) and was immediately transfixed.

As I'll explain in Section 3, I had already devalued much of what was taught at school, but what Godin wrote represented an epiphany. School wasn't just boring and monotonous; it was *stealing dreams*. While school was compulsory, my wife and I committed to rethinking how to best guide our daughters during the hours they were not required to sit in a classroom.

I was so motivated and fired up that I sent Lauren, who was starting her junior year of high school, a link to Godin's e-book. I expected her not to read it, but a few hours later, she came downstairs and said, "I read what you sent, and it blew my mind. I'm now certain that I am not going to college."

Game on.

What drove my conviction: I hope never to forget how I felt when Lauren burst into the room with such conviction. That Saturday morning is when everything you read in this book was implemented with a new level of determination, intentionality, and ferocity.

SEVEN YEARS, FOUR DAYS EACH YEAR

From 2011 through 2017, I facilitated leadership training each July at a four-day leadership camp for eighty to one hundred juniors and seniors in high school with highly diverse backgrounds. Very few knew each other, and the agenda was designed to encourage each kid to "open up." And, wow, did they. During those seven years, I heard hundreds of teenagers repeat—sometimes while crying—the same issues:

- I hate school, other than seeing my friends, but I feel *immense* pressure to excel.
- Everyone tells me I must decide what I want to do for the rest of my life.
- I am highly stressed out about my future.
- I'm being told if I go to college, I can be successful; if I don't, I will always be limited.
- I feel I must go, no matter the cost and debt, which scares the hell out of me.

While I loved interacting with and trying to help those kids, I became extremely frustrated by the pressure from the adults in their lives. Brainwashing them. Scaring the hell out of them. Causing them to take on debt that, for many, would become overwhelming.

What drove my conviction: If a Saturday morning in 2014 is when the implementation of pathbreaker parenting kicked into high gear, those seven years repeatedly emboldened me. Every year, as my daughters entered and advanced through their teenage years, I'd show up, hear the same things, and become angry and (re)motivated all over again.

If you feel strength and conviction in what you've read so far, know that much of it was formed by listening to one teenager after another, in anguish, talk about how they're almost at their wits' end with stress, anxiety, and worry over their futures. And, even worse, they're made to feel that way for no reason.

STAGE 3 CANCER

On April 19, 2018, I received the worst news I had heard until that point. Lauren (at age twenty) had late stage 3 Hodgkin's lymphoma and would need to start a six-month chemotherapy treatment immediately. My child had cancer that could legitimately end her life. We all went through a range of emotions in those first few hours, but during one conversation that evening, she said to me, "Dad, this sucks, but just think how awesome my TED Talk will be."

Figure 7. On the left, Lauren (age twenty) is on the train to work in Washington, DC, after losing her hair during chemotherapy. On the right, she's traveling in Colombia, South America, five years later.

Thankfully, the treatment worked, and she has been cancer-free ever since. On the left, she is on the train to work in Washington, DC, after losing her hair during chemotherapy. She landed her first full-time job two months before the cancer diagnosis and decided not to come home during her fight. She was determined to keep working while pursuing her goals.

On the right, she is (of course) traveling in Colombia, South America, five years later. While on this trip, she (of course) met and made several new friends. One night, they were all on a rooftop talking about life, and each was asked, "If you could go back and change anything in your life, would you?" As part of her answer, she said, "I hope never to have to go through anything like it again, but I would not change my cancer diagnosis. I learned so much about myself by going through that."

It will be a hell of a TED Talk.

What drove my conviction: Again, for the umpteenth time and in the worst way possible, I learned life is entirely unpredictable. Thinking you can plan everything out is fruitless. But, on the flip side, my daughter taught me one thing with complete and final certainty: mindset is *everything*.

ULTIMATUM LEADS TO A TRANSFORMATION

In the fall of 2018 (while her sister was fighting cancer), Brooke decided to give college a try. It didn't go well. She attended for one semester and regressed in virtually every way. After moving back home, she continued to backslide. Sleeping until eleven in the morning. Working part-time at best. Eating junk food and takeout. Although we tried not to apply any pressure (society does plenty of that already), her weight increased noticeably in the twelve months since graduating high school, which we understood exemplified her inner turmoil.

While she was open about not being happy and feeling like she had no real direction, she wasn't taking proactive steps to change her reality. My wife and I agreed we needed to do something and delivered an ultimatum over dinner one night. I'll go into detail in later chapters, but from that moment forward, she found her way.

Figure 8.
On the left, Brooke struggling with direction and confidence at nineteen. On the right, Brooke four years later.

Figure 8 shows Brooke a few weeks before that dinner, then four years later, having lost eighty pounds. There was no "get rich quick" approach, magic diet, or stomach surgery. She transformed her entire existence by applying much of what we had tried to instill in her (we often wondered if it just never landed).

What drove my conviction: As I'll explain in detail, college was the wrong environment for Brooke at that time of her life—as it is for many eighteen-year-olds with no sense of direction. She found her way, step-by-step, by exiting that environment and focusing on herself. Simply put, Brooke's transformation—and how she went about it—was the final inspiration for me to write this book.

"Getting good grades at school means one thing. You are highly proficient at what a now-obsolete system was designed to do—certify someone as ready to be a compliant cog. Is that what you want your teenager to become?"

SECTION 3

THE PATH

The path (cue the ominous music).

It is possible to follow this path and end up perfectly content. It's also possible to bet your life savings at 100-to-1 odds and become rich. But why make that bet if you don't have to?

The path is right for some but unnecessary for most. Might you invest massive amounts of time, energy, stress, money, and anxiety and end up with a thriving young adult? Absolutely. Must you make such an enormous investment to facilitate that outcome? Rarely.

Teenagers and parents are being misled at best and scammed at worst. But because the path is ingrained in our society, you and your teenager must be armed with lots of talking points and self-confidence. To help equip you, let's deconstruct the path step-by-step.

CHAPTER 8

Being a Teenager

Before we start the dismantling, let's quickly agree on something. Do you remember how hard it was to be a teenager? If it feels impossible to recreate the rawness of your emotions when you were sixteen years old, spend an hour online doing a search such as "What is it like to be a teenager?" and it will come back to you.

Daily Life ◇ Parenting

The Teenage Years: 10 Struggles Only a Teenager Understands

Being Stuck Between Childhood and Adulthood	Caring What Others Think
Parent Lectures (and Nagging)	Relentless Academic Pressure
Pimples First Kiss, First Crush, First Heartbreak	Peer Pressure on a Whole New Level
	Friend Drama
Feeling Pressured (and Totally Clueless) About Their Future	Mood Swings

Figure 9. The teenage years are uniquely difficult, with many internal and external pressures.

(Source: Nancy Reynolds, "The Teenage Years: 10 Struggles Only a Teenager Understands," *Raising Teens Today*, July 5, 2020.)

The pressure to conform starts as early as twelve years old and, for many, does not stop even as young adults.

Declarative statements about the importance of high achievement form a powder keg of pressure. "Your future success and happiness are at stake. What you do now is a harbinger of what you can become. Picking the right career is critical. One wrong decision could ruin your life."

And the questions come at them daily. Did you do your homework? Did you study for your test? Did you finish your project? Did you practice your presentation? Did you fill out that application? Have you decided where you want to go to college? What about your major? Any idea what you want to do with your life?

I promise you one thing. You can only hold breakthrough dialogues by first internalizing the realization that your teenager struggles with the very nature of being a teenager. Even with zero external pressure, they're a hot mess at times. But if you make declarative statements and apply unceasing pressure, they will almost certainly shut down on you.

Please think about that.

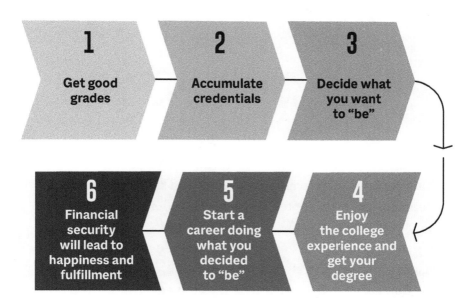

CHAPTER 9

Get Good Grades

Much of a teenager's mindset, psyche, and self-assessment centers on a widely accepted and rarely questioned norm in our society (and many others). *Go to school and get good grades.* It is, by far, the topic that infiltrates interactions between parents and teenagers. Did you do well on your test? Will you get an A in that class? Can you do extra credit to pull your grade up? Are you doing everything you can to keep your perfect GPA?

In the next section, I will share the mindset we established with our daughters starting in middle school, but for now, let's focus on what's being asked of teenagers and why. To do that, I will lean on the brilliant thought starter I mentioned earlier, called *Stop Stealing Dreams* by Seth Godin, and the single question he repeatedly comes back to.

What is school for?

While I highly recommend you read Godin's manifesto, I will share a few passages and my commentary, as I vividly remember its impact on me.[1]

Godin starts with why school was created, when, and by whom.

> *It wasn't until 1918 that nationwide compulsory education was in place.*

> *Part of the rationale used to sell this major transformation to industrialists was the idea that educated kids would actually become **more compliant and productive workers**. Our current system of teaching kids to sit in straight rows and obey instructions isn't a coincidence—it was an investment in our economic future. The plan: trade short-term child-labor wages for longer-term productivity by **giving kids a head-start in doing what they're told**.*

> *Large-scale education was not developed to motivate kids or to create scholars. It was invented to **churn out adults who worked well within the system**. Scale was more important than quality, just as it was for most industrialists. Of course, it worked. **Several generations of productive, fully employed workers followed**.*

---

1 All of the following passages from the manifesto are used by permission from Seth Godin and taken from *Stop Stealing Dreams* (2014), https://seths.blog/wp-content/uploads/2014/09/stop-stealing-dreams-print.pdf. Boldface emphasis added.

Have you ever wondered why school was created, by whom, when, and for what purpose? Up until September 2014, I hadn't either. The business case for school—the ROI, if you will—was based on two desired outcomes.

- Create a place where parents can send their kids while they work (factories need workers).
- Over several years, "teach" the kids to become compliant and productive workers.

As Godin states, the goal was never to motivate kids or to create scholars. You went to school, became certified as ready to work, and got a job at a local factory or business. Make no mistake, that is why school was created.

> *Culture changes to match the economy, not the other way around. The economy needed an institution that would churn out compliant workers, so we built it.* **Factories didn't happen because there were schools; schools happened because there were factories.**
>
> *The reason so many people grow up to look for a job is that* **the economy has needed people who would grow up to look for a job.**

It doesn't happen overnight; instead, it's a slow drip through a purpose-built system that kids are forced to attend for over a decade. They're repeatedly told it's all for their benefit—a free service that certifies one to get and keep a job. A good job. A steady job. The higher your grades, the better the job you can get. And, of course, parents can pay extra money for more advanced versions of school, which will enhance their child's ability to get the best jobs. Kids work their way through the system, become adults who get jobs, and send their kids to school while doing those jobs.

While the system is now largely self-perpetuating, it is critical to maintain order and keep everyone on schedule. How do you do that? Fear.

> *The shortcut to compliance, then, isn't to reason with someone, to outline the options, and to sell a solution. No,* **the shortcut is to induce fear, to activate the amygdala.** *Do this or we'll laugh at you, expel you, tell your parents, make you sit in the corner. Do this or you will get a bad grade, be suspended, never amount to anything.* **Do this or you are in trouble.**
>
> **It goes further than merely ensuring classroom comportment.** *Fear is used to ensure that no one stretches too far, questions the status quo, or makes a ruckus.* **Fear** *is reinforced in career planning, in academics, and even in interpersonal interactions.* **Fear** *lives in the guidance office, too.*
>
> *The message is simple:* **better fit in or you won't get into a good school.** *If you get into a good school and do what they say, you'll get a good job, and you'll be fine. But if you don't—***it'll go on your permanent record.**

Yes, to some extent, fear must be used to maintain order. Without rules within a system with tens of millions of participants, chaos ensues. I get and accept that, but the use of fear at school goes far beyond just maintaining order. Teenagers are stressed, anxious, and afraid because they're constantly told there will be devastating consequences in the future if they do not comply in the present. And that brings us back to the maniacal obsession with good grades.

*It's clear that **the economy has changed**. What we want and expect from our best citizens has changed. Not only in what we do when we go to our jobs, but also in the doors that have been opened for people who want to make an impact on our culture.*

*At the very same time, **the acquisition of knowledge has been forever transformed by the Internet**, the most efficient and powerful information delivery system ever developed. The change in the economy and the delivery of information online combine to amplify the speed of change. **These rapid cycles are overwhelming the ability of the industrialized system of education to keep up**.*

*Amplified by the Web and the connection revolution, **human beings are no longer rewarded most for work as compliant cogs**. Instead, **our chaotic world is open to the work of passionate individuals, intent on carving their own paths**.*

Getting good grades at school means one thing. You are highly proficient at what a now-obsolete system was designed to do—certify someone as ready to be a compliant cog. Is that what you want your teenager to become? Godin is not alone in this point of view. As Taylor Pearson states in his book, *The End of Jobs: Money, Meaning and Freedom Without the 9-to-5*, what so many parents seek for their teenagers—the safety and security of getting (and keeping) a good job—is increasingly obsolete.

"Jobs were safe in a world where more and more were being created and wages were increasing—which they were for most of the 20th century. Since around 1980, that hasn't been the case."

Figure 10. The job market started to change in 1980, and those changes were amplified by the internet.

(Source: Taylor Pearson, *The End of Jobs: Money, Meaning and Freedom Without the 9-to-5*, 2015, p. 209.)

When people talk about the "tight labor market" or how "wages are not keeping up with housing costs," keep Pearson's statement in mind. Your local, national, and global economy has dramatically changed in less than one generation, and the pace will continue unabated. When you insist your teenager excel in a system that reached obsolescence years ago and loses ground yearly, you set them up to be wholly unprepared to navigate and flourish when "human beings are no longer rewarded most for work as compliant cogs" (as stated by Godin in the passage above).

THE INTERNET CHANGED EVERYTHING

Today's parents experienced a seismic event over the last twenty-five years that fundamentally changed our lives. Think about how different the world we live in today is from just a generation ago.

For example, think about how you accessed information when you were in middle or high school. When I was that age, there were three channels on TV, one local newspaper, and a few magazines my parents subscribed to that did not interest me. If I wanted to access information of my own volition, I had to leave my house and try to find it. I'd go to a bookstore or library, ask for guidance, and likely end up reading an encyclopedia or browsing through something called microfiche. Information was hard to find, what you located was hard to filter through, and the format was not compelling (video was rare).

What did that mean? From the standpoint of accessing information, school was the only game in town. You showed up for several hours, received some information, and went home. When not at school, you didn't think, "Hmm, I feel motivated to learn ____ right now" because you had no natural ability to do so. You let someone else tell you what to learn, when to learn, and how to learn it. You had no choice in the matter.

But then the internet happened, and access to information changed forever. It transformed from being hard to get to instantly accessible, easily searchable, filtered, and highly specific. In minutes, I can choose what I want to learn and my preferred medium to learn it. I can read it, watch it, listen to it, and/or discuss it. And yet, remarkably, parents continue to pressure their teenagers to excel at memorizing and regurgitating information others tell them is meaningful.

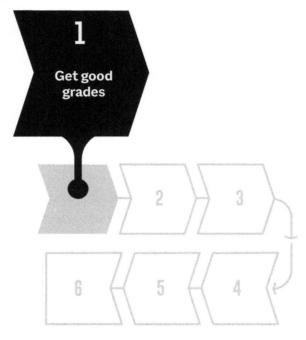

Godin titled his manifesto *Stop Stealing Dreams* for a reason. Not only is school—and the pursuit of excellence within it—obsolete in today's post-industrial revolution world, it uses fear to paralyze teenagers and prevent them from dreaming. In a world where anyone with an internet connection is empowered to pursue their hopes and dreams at their own pace, confidently chart their own course, and evaluate, challenge, or even choose not to participate in any system, parents send their kids to school and insist they "get good grades" in topics and subject matter of no interest to them.

Instead of demonstrating constant curiosity and a desire to explore, teenagers conform. If they choose to explore on their own and only study enough to get a C on a test, they're told to shape up and focus. This maniacal obsession turns them into followers who wait to be told what direction to go next and strips them of the confidence to self-direct their learning about subjects, events, or potential ways to generate income. With that, I leave you with one final quote from Godin's manifesto.

> *There really are only two tools available to the educator.* ***The easy one is fear. Fear is easy to awake, easy to maintain, but ultimately toxic. The other tool is passion.*** *A kid in love with dinosaurs or baseball or earth science is going to learn it on her own. She's going to push hard for ever more information, and better still, master the thinking behind it.*

> *The problem is that **individual passion is hard to scale—** hard to fit into the industrial model. It's not reliably ignited. It's **certainly harder to create for large masses of people**. Sure, it's easy to get a convention center filled with delegates to chant for a candidate, and easier still to engage the masses at Wembley Stadium, but **the passion that fuels dreams and creates change must come from the individual, not from a demigod.***

CHAPTER 10

Accumulate Credentials

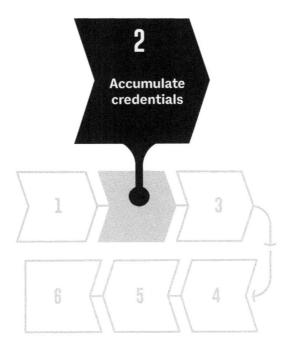

Credential: a qualification, achievement, personal quality, or aspect of a person's background, typically when used to indicate that they are suitable for something

Being suitable for something. That is what teenagers are told to focus on.

Back in the day, that "something" was a steady job and decent living, both accessible with the free high school diploma available to everyone. Things were simpler back then, but the goalposts moved as new social classes emerged and white-collar jobs expanded.

College morphed from higher education for the elite to accessible postsecondary education for many. And the "something" to become suitable for shifted from a steady job and a decent living to a high-paying job and a potentially extravagant living. Sure, a high school diploma equipped you for blue-collar work, but a college degree offered the eligibility to pursue financial success without limitations. Not surprisingly, the goalposts moved again.

In 1950, around one-third of those twenty-five or older had a high school degree, while less than one in ten had a college degree. By the early 2000s, almost ninety percent graduated from high school, and more than one in three had a college degree. Instead of tens of thousands of new college graduates entering the workforce each year, it was millions. A high school diploma was now virtually irrelevant because everyone had one, and a college degree was no longer an automatic ticket to the upper echelons of the corporate world. And so, yet again, the goalposts moved.

Eligibility to maximize one's success now requires a "selective" college degree—because anyone can get a "regular" college degree. And that, combined with the proliferation of social media, has led to an ever-increasing arms race over the last two decades. When did you last see a parent post that their kid will attend a community college in the fall? I'm guessing you can't think of a single example because most parents and teenagers are determined to attend a college with a name they can brag about.

Good grades? Please. That is now table stakes. Being suitable for success now demands not just multiple credentials but the most impressive ones possible. With that in mind, let me ask you a question. What do you do when something is important to you, and your decision is centered on validating a person or group of people's ability to deliver what you want? For example, what do you do when hiring a babysitter, painter, plumber, or interior designer, or when contemplating the cost of tickets for a concert, sporting event, or play?

Let me guess—the first thing you do is check if the babysitter graduated from a prestigious babysitting school, if the interior designer graduated from a prestigious trade school, or if the performers/players/entertainers graduated from a prestigious acting or music school. Isn't that what's important to you? Their credentials?

Of course, I'm being facetious because none of us do that.

Instead, we all request a referral, check online reviews, and/or pay attention to word of mouth. You hire the babysitter if a friend says they're reliable and responsible. You hire the interior designer if their work in a neighbor's house blows you away. And you buy tickets to the show if reviews insist it's terrific. When you observe outstanding work with your own eyes or when trusted peers recommend a person, product, or service, you don't waste time vetting credentials because they're irrelevant. Right?

Then why do you believe (or convince yourself) that decisions like these differ from how "businesspeople" make the same choices? You don't insist someone responsible for your child's safety and well-being have a degree from a babysitting school. Do you think a businessperson seeking to hire someone to analyze data, run marketing campaigns, or sell products cares if a candidate has a degree from a prestigious business school? The dirty little secret no one talks about is—they don't. And, if they do, see section 5 where I'll share how I guided our daughters to deal with such people.

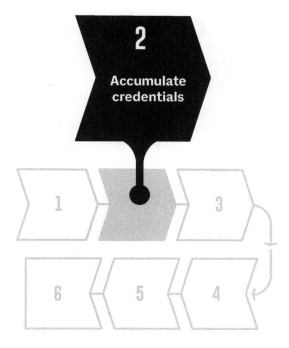

As you consider the first two steps on the path, do you start to empathize with your teenager? Do you understand why they shut down? Is it difficult for them to enjoy playing a sport or acting in a play because of internalized pressure to excel? Are they often aloof and tired? Anxious? Jittery?

Every July for seven years, I heard the outpouring of emotions all this caused. I listened to teenagers hindered by the sheer number of tasks they were expected to complete and how they were being pressured to excel at everything they did. Even worse, the emphasis on getting good grades and hoarding credentials wasn't even the most destructive thing being done to them.

CHAPTER 11

Decide What You Want to Be

Okay, lots of bad vibes in those last few chapters; sorry, I'm being such a downer. Let's shift gears and talk about something positive!

When I turned twenty-two, a mutual friend invited Donna, a girl I didn't know, to my birthday party. My friend was about to give up when I stepped away from dancing (terribly) to Marky Mark and the Funky Bunch, grabbed the phone, and thought, "I'll talk her into it." I gave it everything I had—all my best charm and coaxing powers (the words "Sugar Bear" came into play multiple

Figure 11. My wife, Donna, and me about fifteen minutes after we met for the first time.

times). She was a tough sell, but this picture was taken about an hour later, when I met her for the first time (I know, cool shirt).

Five days later, on the Wednesday before Thanksgiving, we went on our first date, and what was supposed to be one hour turned into four. When I got home that night, I told Mom, "I think I just had lunch with the girl I'm gonna marry." We've been together ever since, married twenty-eight years with two daughters. True story.

A split-second decision changed everything, and I never saw it coming. With that in mind, take a few minutes and think about how your life has unfolded from when you were a teenager or young adult to now. Think about the decisions you made (and didn't make) that impacted your life today.

Happiness. Primary relationship (if you're in one). Financial situation. Health. Children (if you have any). Friendships. Hobbies. Job(s). Where you live and, living arrangements. How much money you've saved. Passions. Relationships with your parents and siblings. It is daunting, right?

Countless decisions and outcomes could have gone either way. Some decisions felt monumental, only to end up being irrelevant. Others (like grabbing a phone and calling someone Sugar Bear) felt inconsequential, only to change your entire life trajectory. It happens to us all—good, bad, and indifferent. We make choices that unpredictably impact our lives and must navigate the consequences, opportunities, and unforeseeable scenarios caused by the choices of others. I encourage you to remember this when trying to preordain your teenager's future.

As you think about your past choices, consider the significant decisions you could pressure your teenager to make and stick with long term, such as:

- Where will you live when you're forty?
- Who will be your best friend when you're thirty?
- Will you have children, and if so, how many will you have?
- What two hobbies will you commit to be good at as an adult?
- Will you get married, and if so, who will you marry?
- Etc.

Do you insist your teenager decide huge things like this? Of course you don't. Except you do. There is one teeny, tiny, long-term decision you beseech your teenager to make.

What do you want to be?

How could your teenager be anything but virtually paralyzed by such a question? And why do you believe they must answer it by the arbitrary age of nineteen or twenty?

Simple. Because the college industry wouldn't have much to offer if the approach was to show up for four years, have a great time, learn some random stuff, and then decide what kind of job you want after graduation. That is far from a strong enough value proposition to warrant several years and gobs of money. Instead, the college industry's pitch is "Pick a major, and we will give you the necessary credentials, network, and knowledge to get a job doing what you choose." Ding, ding! That sounds a lot better, right?

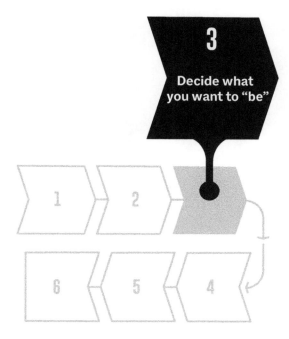

3

Decide what you want to "be"

Risking political incorrectness, why are arranged marriages in other countries the worst thing ever, but forcing a teenager, with zero real-world life or work experience, to decide what they will want to "be" or "do" as a career makes complete sense? These teenagers are expected to predict their future responsibilities, challenges, wants, needs, and dreams, even though they are all likely to change significantly over the coming years.

Long before our daughters started high school, my wife and I decided, "Nope, this is dumb." Rather than insist they pick a specific major or career, we encouraged them to develop transferable skills and only worry about one thing: What do you want to try first? We will go deep in the last two sections, but we're only halfway done dismantling the path.

CHAPTER 12

College

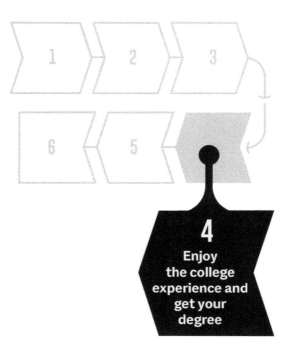

People can be highly emotional and defensive about college, which I get. When you invest what's required to earn a college degree, you identify strongly with that investment and don't respond well to someone telling you it doesn't matter. And it does matter. It signifies something; for many people, it is a tremendous accomplishment that warrants celebrating.

With that said, we now live in a world where the value proposition of paying for information, a network, and credentials has never made less sense. In parallel, the cost of doing so has never been higher.

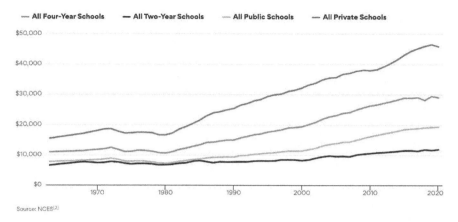

Average Total Cost of College by School Type, 1963-2020

— All Four-Year Schools — All Two-Year Schools — All Public Schools — All Private Schools

Source: NCES[2]

Figure 12. Even when adjusting for inflation, the cost of a college degree has tripled in the last forty years.

(Source: Jessica Bryant, "Cost of College over Time: Rising Tuition Statistics," *Best Colleges,* January 12, 2023.)

We never eliminated college as an option for our daughters; one of them went to college (she dropped out after one semester—I'll explain later). But we did have lots of conversations about the concept of opportunity cost, which I'll detail in the last two sections. You can invest gobs of money and a 1,000-plus days over four years *or* apply your time and money differently.

Rather than embrace the tried-and-true response "College isn't for everyone," I encourage a mindset of "College is only for some people" as you vet the decision using two words. First, the word *only*. Is college the *only* option after high school? Is it the *only* place to form lifelong friendships and have lots of fun? The *only* way to build a network? The *only* opportunity to expand one's mind and learn wonderfully exciting things? It will require little conversation or thought to confidently answer each question with a "no." Next, revisit each question, replace the word *only* with *best*, and consider the four typical hoped-for college outcomes. Experience. Growth. Network. Degree (i.e., credential).

EXPERIENCE

College is presented as a once-in-a-lifetime opportunity to venture off on your own, enjoy a new sense of independence, meet new people, and create lasting friendships. For those fortunate enough to go, it's a rite of passage. I hear it all the time—"College is awesome! There's just nothing like it. I will not deprive my child of the opportunity to have such an amazing experience. I will invest and spend whatever it takes. If necessary, I will take on debt or encourage my child to do so."

And my response is always the same. I'm not anti-college for everyone, but it's irresponsible to assume any one experience is *best* for all. For example, four months after graduating high school, Lauren wrote a blog post saying, "Trust me, a full-moon party in Bali with people from all over the world is a lot more fun than a sweaty frat house."

Figure 13. Lauren in Bali, Indonesia, four months after her high school graduation.

Two months later, she lived in San Francisco for three months while participating in a program called UnCollege with about twenty other people. They were all bucking the mainstream trend of attending college after high school, and the bonds they built remain strong today.

Figure 14. Lauren (third from the left in checked pants) in San Francisco, California, six months after her high school graduation.

Lauren's sister, Brooke, was nowhere near ready to travel by herself to a developing country or live in San Francisco with a bunch of people she didn't know. She was utterly different from Lauren. She decided to try college because it was what all her friends were doing and she couldn't come up with a better option. Four months later, she quit.

> College in general gave me anxiety because I felt like I didn't have the motivation or confidence to be there. At that time in my life, college just wasn't the right environment for me to flourish at all. I just kind of floundered.

When I asked Brooke why she dropped out after one semester, that is what she said. When I asked for a bit more detail, she said this.

> I felt overwhelmed by the "college culture" (meeting tons of new people, living in an insanely nasty, gross, and old dorm room, all of the events like homecoming, new student meetings, etc.) and it felt like I woke up every day and just had to go do shit I didn't want to do to "fit in." I was very unhappy.

College was an unhealthy environment at that stage of Brooke's life. She went to college lacking motivation and direction, and the lack of both worsened each time we saw her during that one semester. She seemed unsettled and wasn't gushing about all the fun she was having, the friends she was making, or what she was learning. But it was deeper than that—she was regressing. We knew it, and she knew it. By Thanksgiving, she decided she would finish the semester and drop out.

The classic response is, "Lots of kids feel this way at the start of college. Rather than make a hasty decision to quit, she should have stuck with it. She would have matured by working through her insecurities and eventually found direction." I hope you're not that assumptive.

I understand many kids struggle in their first semester at college—with loneliness, depression, imposter syndrome, all kinds of things—and some work through it and thrive. I get that. But for Brooke and millions of other kids, college is *not* and will *not* be a wonderful experience. The high-activity, crowded environment is overwhelming. The "weight" of what has been and is being invested to be at college represents crushing pressure to present as "I'm having the time of my life—this is *so* worth it." The lack of direction and a known purpose lead to bad habits.

Please don't be the socially conscious parent who defaults to a "college experience or bust" mentality. Many students enjoy college, but the reality you must accept as a parent is that the experience is "only for some people."

GROWTH

College is presented as an enriching environment in which you break away from your parents, learn how to take care of yourself, and transition into adulthood. And, again, some participants do exactly that. But, have you ever stopped to consider what type of circumstances typically best enable one to grow and develop? Is it commonly a busy atmosphere teeming with noise, people, and activity? Is it usually a setting where a significant portion of your time is spent on fulfilling assignments given by others? Does it usually involve a continuous stream of deadlines?

I'm sure it's possible to thrive in environments like these. Still, I believe self-development comes down to one critical element— an environment in which there is adequate space, freedom, and time for deep introspection and exploration of what causes me and only me to feel accomplished and fulfilled. College students rarely engage in such introspection and exploration. Instead, they exist in an activity-rich, deadline-heavy, crowded bubble for four years. Upon graduating, they walk across a stage, get their diploma, and are required to shift into the fast-paced, career-driven world of adulting, where they're expected to pursue success. Many wake up a few years later wondering, "Who am I? What am I even doing?"

Does this happen to every college graduate? Of course not. But, as I shared at the start of this book, young adults in our society are increasingly unhappy and lack fulfillment. As an environment fostering growth and development, college is "only for some people."

NETWORK

When I graduated from college in 1994, I could not connect and network with everyone my parents, friends, and parents of friends knew. It wasn't like I could sit down with my Dad and ask, "Can you write down the name, title, company, and contact information for everyone you know in the business world?" But today, I can instantly search for, connect with, and start a dialogue with anyone. I can join a meet-up an hour from now and try to create mutual value with a particular group of individuals. I can find tens of people already doing any job, reach out, and ask them what they like and dislike about it. If I'm pursuing an opportunity or role with a specific company, I can immediately find everyone in my first- and second-degree network who works there.

For example, Lauren has a business network of more than four hundred contacts (and counting). She didn't attend college, so how did she build this network? If you visit her LinkedIn page (https://www.linkedin.com/in/laurenmarlowe/), you will see this quote from George McKerrow, CEO of Ted's Montana Grill:

> *"Lauren is a dynamic, bold and gregarious young lady that loves adventure and new experiences. She is creative and excels at whatever job she tackles. She has compassion and passion for her fellow human beings as well as for her life. Lauren will make a mark wherever she goes."*

Nine months after high school, Lauren was a server when the restaurant debuted, and Mr. McKerrow visited. Because she was taught (and had practiced) how to walk up to an adult, introduce herself, and initiate a conversation, that's what she did. The conversation was short, but a positive impression was made. The next time he returned, Lauren walked over to say hello, and they had another brief conversation. Each time he returned, he requested her as his server, and they would catch up. A few months later, Lauren asked if he'd be open to writing a referral letter, as she was about to start her career. He said he'd be happy to; the quote above is from that letter.

Is the quote general in nature? Yes. Did he have his assistant write it? Maybe. Would that letter ever land her a job on its own? Nah, probably not, unless she applied for a corporate job at Ted's. But that isn't the point. The point is that anyone can learn to network with some coaching and practice. It's not complicated. Better yet, building a network while not at college has two huge upsides.

First, at college, you build an initial network with people mostly your age and with no real-world experience (other than some professors and guest speakers). From the jump, because she didn't go to college and chose to travel a lot, Lauren built a uniquely diverse network of people: from young to old, from no real-world experience to forty years of it, from all walks of life and around the world. She leverages that network both professionally and personally, and there are numerous countries she can travel to and know someone. You do not build a network like that in college.

Second, Lauren was strongly encouraged to network with recruiters and proactively did so when starting her career at twenty. By the time she was twenty-two, when most of her friends were graduating college with no recruiters in their network, she had relationships with several intelligent, connected recruiters who knew her to be a strong candidate. Already with three years of experience under her belt, she scored her dream job at twenty-three through, you guessed it, a recruiter.

The network you create in college can be helpful "for some people." But is college necessary to build an impactful network? Goodness, no.

DEGREE

A favorite podcast of mine is *How I Built This*, hosted by Guy Raz, in which he interviews company founders. Each episode walks through everything: how the initial idea was spawned, the motivation to start the business, the early challenges, and how the business eventually scaled. One episode was about Audible.com, founded in 1997 and sold to Amazon in 2008 for $300 million.

Don Katz was a freelance writer for *Rolling Stone* magazine when he founded Audible.com at age forty-three. As shared on the podcast, he lacked "tech" knowledge, leadership experience, an entrepreneurial mindset, and capital (other than credit cards). Stop and think about that. He decided to start a company while lacking *all* those traits.

Amazon acquires Audible for $300 million

The deal for the audiobook seller, another indicator of the online retailer's confidence in the digital-content market, is expected to close midyear.

Caroline McCarthy 🐦

Jan. 31, 2008 7:59 a.m. PT

Figure 15. Don Katz ended up selling the company he started, despite not having the "required" knowledge or credentials, for $300 million.

(Source: Caroline McCarthy, "Amazon Acquires Audible for $300 million," *CNET*, January 31, 2008.)

Why did he take such a monumental leap? Because he was a long-distance runner and hated carrying and changing cassettes while on a long run. And, once he became motivated enough to solve that problem, he created, scaled, and sold his business for $300 million after eleven years. Most businesses never reach that kind of success, and I don't listen to this podcast because I hope to find a "get rich quick" idea. Instead, I find this podcast fascinating because you consistently hear three things from the founders being interviewed.

First, in almost every situation, the founder(s) knew very little about the potential solution to the problem; they were just highly energized to solve it. Second, they sold out and put everything they had into solving this problem. It became their why. Third, they either learned what they needed to know as they went or sought out the expertise of others.

I turned both of my daughters on to this podcast as teenagers because it fosters a mindset that, more than ever, no credentials or prior experience are needed. If you become determined to do something, you'll figure it out, and—because of this thing called the internet—there are countless ways to learn what you need to know and find people who can do what you cannot do.

This thinking invites a classic debate I've participated in multiple times. The first response is typically, "Granted, anyone can start a company without a college degree, but what about someone who wants to land a high-paying corporate job? Those jobs require a college degree."

Except they (almost always) don't. A company is just a collection of people with needs and goals; just like you, when they need to hire someone, they rarely seek or value a credential. They leverage their network and ask for recommendations. As we'll discuss in the following two sections, between the ages of eighteen and twenty-two (or any age range), rather than get a certification (i.e., a college degree), it's far more valuable to build a growth mindset, a "portfolio" of your work, and a strong network of people who will validate what's in that portfolio. When you show up for an interview, you want to say, "Here is the work I've done to date, here is how it relates to the work you need to be done, and here are three people you know who will verify my work and attitude."

This advice typically elicits a response like, "You're wrong. Companies make it very clear in their job descriptions that a college degree is required for most good jobs. But even if you're lucky enough to land a high-paying job without a degree, you'll get stuck. You'll need a degree to be promoted past a certain level." Perhaps, but stop for a moment and think about a scenario.

Suppose you work with a highly respected, superstar coworker being considered for promotion to leadership. Imagine this person is not promoted, and when you ask why, you're told, "Everyone views her as an up-and-coming leader who would be a tremendous asset to our management team. But unfortunately, we cannot promote her because we have a policy that our leaders must have a college degree." How would you feel about that response? It sounds so shallow and dumb when you say it out loud, right? Would you want to commit your allegiance to a company with such a policy?

"Well, Seth, rules are rules," I often hear. "The companies have the power; they set the rules, and those that follow them get ahead." Nope. It is not 1985 anymore. That mindset will set your teenager up to be taken advantage of for as long as they decide to work for a company.

The internet changed everything. The economy works differently than it did before globalization. The job market works differently than it did one generation ago. Companies do not have the same power over employees that they once did because everyone now has unlimited alternatives (if they dare to pursue them). There are tens of millions of companies, hundreds of millions of jobs, and countless ways to deliver and be paid for value creation. And they are all in your teenager's purview.

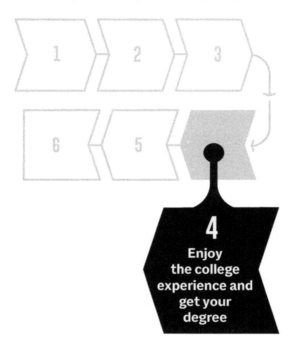

Many teenagers venture off to college and live fulfilling and happy lives. But why make such a critical decision in a vacuum? Money, time, and opportunity costs matter. College is one option, but your teenager can likely attain an equal or better result without the massive investment in time, money, stress, and expectations. And, of course, for many teenagers, college isn't just unnecessary; it is damaging.

Your teenager is looking at you for direction; please don't squash their ability to dream and design an option that best fits their DNA. Don't allow the lazy mindset of doing what everyone else does because it's convenient or safe. Be better than that. Be more interesting than that.

CHAPTER 13

Start a Career

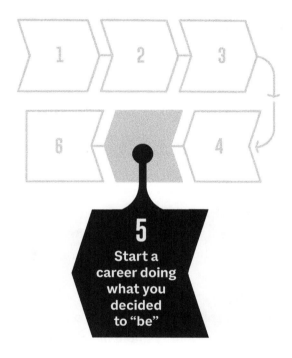

5
Start a career doing what you decided to "be"

When college graduates walk off the stage with a degree, they often feel ready to take on the world. Finally, after eight to ten years of blood, sweat, and tears, they're certified as "suitable for something." They have proof of being persistent, hardworking, task-oriented, and knowledgeable about a specific area of focus (i.e., their major). Potential employers will not only tune in to their loud and bright signal, they will seek it because most of them require it.

Unfortunately, as I mentioned, it is not 1985 anymore. The economy and job market have dramatically changed and will continue to do so.

And college graduates are facing the increasingly harsh reality that a college degree doesn't carry the significance it once did. For many roles, it has no importance.

There are two job openings for every unemployed American. So why are recent graduates struggling to get hired?

Updated Feb 21, 2023

Figure 16. A recent study details college graduates' tremendous struggles when starting their careers.

(Source: Ryan McGonagill, "There Are Two Job Openings for Every Unemployed American. So Why Are Recent Graduates Struggling to Get Hired?," *Business.com*, February 21, 2023.)

A recently conducted Business.com study shines a glaring spotlight on this reality. Armed with strong academic records, some work/internship experience, and professionally polished résumés, four college graduates sent out hundreds of applications for mostly entry-level jobs. Here are the results:[2]

- Three hundred applications sent.
- Ninety percent of applications did not get a response.
- Two percent of applications resulted in an interview.
- Not a single application led to employment.

The four of them went 0 for 300, which the author concluded was "eye-opening." I highly recommend reading the article and viewing

---

2 Ryan McGonagill, "There Are Two Job Openings for Every Unemployed American. So Why Are Recent Graduates Struggling to Get Hired?," *Business.com*, February 21, 2023, https://www.business.com/hiring/new-graduates-job-search-experiment/.

the accompanying twenty-five-minute video in which the four college graduates advise their peers as follows:

- "Get as much experience and build as many relationships as you can."
- "Do as much face-to-face networking as possible."
- "Companies are making it exceedingly difficult to meet their requirements."
- "You have to find ways to showcase your skills and what you have to offer."
- "You really have to learn to market yourself."

This study frustrated me because these young adults were terribly misled. They were told a college degree would set them apart, only to learn everyone they're competing against has the same credentials. They were told not to worry about getting experience, only to learn hiring managers value experience above all else. They were told a college degree is the requirement, only to be told they're not fulfilling what's required. They were told the network they built in college would open doors, only to discover they must aggressively market themselves.

What a college degree supposedly signals—things like work ethic, maturity, knowledge, and persistence—no longer sets anyone apart. Their signal falls on deaf ears because millions of other college graduates are sending out the same signal and applying for the same jobs in the same way (online applications). While sitting in classrooms, studying for tests, and going to parties, these four college graduates were not doing what they're now being told matters. They were not gaining on-the-job experience, fostering an active network of experienced people, or building a portfolio showcasing in-demand work.

HOW HIRING WORKS

Let's discuss how hiring works. I've interviewed hundreds of potential candidates for numerous positions. When assessing a candidate, I might start with a short conversation in which I ask a few simple questions to gauge their maturity, mindset, and communication skills. But some people are great interviewers only to become bad employees. I need to know more.

I would want to spend additional time reviewing a portfolio showcasing their experience, knowledge, and work product. Why? A résumé or credential tells me almost nothing because everybody has one. I prefer that a candidate show me their work because that will give me great insight into (1) what they can and cannot (yet) do well and (2) how persistent, creative, and unique they are in building their portfolio. And, last, I would try to find someone in my network to validate a candidate's work ethic, persistence, attitude, coachability, and so forth. Straightforward enough, right?

Now, what do those steps require? An hour or more of my time for each candidate. And, because open positions are posted online, how many applications do most jobs get today? Hundreds, if not thousands. Can I, or anyone else seeking to hire someone, dedicate hundreds of hours to the process? Of course not. And that is why meaningless requirements are listed in job descriptions. Allow me to explain.

Again, I can't say it enough: a company is a collection of people with needs and goals. Individual people (called hiring managers) provide their needs for a specific job to Human Resources (now commonly referred to as the People Team or Talent Acquisition Team), who create a job description like the one in Figure 17. The description lists many capabilities and skills, but the first two are "bachelor's degree" and "3+ years of experience."

A hiring manager rarely, if ever, insists on a college degree when hiring. Remember: when you say it out loud, it sounds dumb and shallow. Instead, Human Resources adds "bachelor's degree" and "x number of years of experience" before submitting the description and posting the job. Why? In 1985, job postings were local and might get a few applicants. But today, job postings are global, and the only way to process all of them is to add filters with a yes or no answer. *That* is why you're being told a college degree is required for most high-paying

Required

> • Bachelor's degree in a relevant field preferred (Human-Computer Interaction, information design, communications, Computer Systems, etc.)

• 3+ years of experience in UI/UX design
• Proficiency using UX and protyping tools (Axure, Sketch, Adobe Creative Cloud, InVision, etc.)
• Experience with WCAG accessibility standards
• Proven effectiveness in working as a member in cross-functional teams which include business analysts, designers, researchers, developers, and product owners
• Experience with Agile and/or lean philosophy and methods
• Design experience for both web and mobile
• Ability to create wireframes as well as visual design comps
• Portfolio examples of sketches, workflows, interactions, and end state work
• Up-to-date with the latest UI trends, techniques, and technologies
• A user-centered approach in design perspective and practice
• Excellent verbal and written communication skills
• Positive attitude and be able to work effectively in a team
• Strong sense of accountability and drive to get results
• High attention to detail but able to work quickly to meet deadlines
• Ability to solve problems creatively and effectively
• Maintain a user-centered approach in design perspective and practice
• Must be legally authorized to work in the United States for any employer without sponsorship
• Successful completion of interview required to meet job qualification
• Reliable, punctual attendance is an essential function of the position

Preferred

• IAirline experience
• Preferred CISSP, CISA, or CISM
• Understanding of HTML, JavaScript & CSS

Figure 17. The actual job description for the role Lauren now holds at a Fortune 200 company.

jobs. It isn't because anyone believes a college degree is the only way to validate what kind of an employee you will be. It's because it's convenient.

I've talked with several people from Human Resources about this. We end up in the same place within three questions.

Question #1—Suppose you find a candidate to be outstanding. She shares a portfolio showcasing advanced capabilities to do the work needed, presents herself exceedingly well, and is highly recommended. In that scenario, would you care if she has a college degree? One hundred percent of the time, the answer is, "In that scenario, no, I wouldn't."

Question #2—Then why list a college degree as a requirement? The answer almost always starts with "A college degree has merit. It signals that a person is persistent and achieved a hard milestone or has specific knowledge we need, etc." I almost always get some version of that kind of response, which leads to the third and final question.

Question #3—I agree that a college degree is one potential signal a person has those traits, but if it isn't the *only* way, why make it a requirement? Checkmate.

This isn't me saying Human Resources teams are full of bad people—not at all. They have aggressive hiring quotas, are typically understaffed, and must find ways to process many tasks and fill roles as quickly as possible. I get it. However, because I know this is how the process works, our daughters were taught a better way to get a job, which I will explain later.

College graduates struggle because they accumulate knowledge and credentials that opt them in according to system-based filters that mean very little to today's hiring managers. Very few companies have—as part of their bylaws or About Us pages—policies that "require" a college degree to work there. And, if a company does have such a dumb and shallow policy, go work at one of the tens of millions of companies that do not.

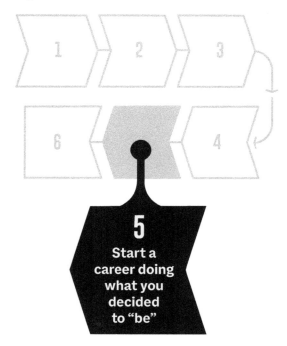

5

Start a career doing what you decided to "be"

College graduates go 0 for 300 when competing against hundreds of people with the same credentials because they lack the proof of value creation and soft skills that are in high demand with hiring managers. But you can prevent your teenager from facing such a reality as a young adult, and I'll walk you through it step-by-step in this book's last section.

CHAPTER 14

Financial Security, Happiness, and Fulfillment

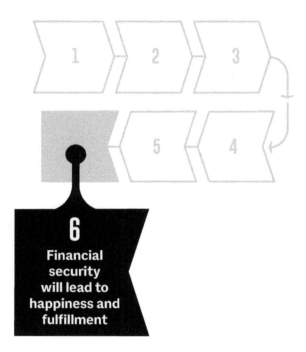

Not only do college graduates believe their degree will land them a job, but that their conformity will lead to a giant treasure chest at the end of the rainbow. When they consider what was invested, how could it not?

In the previous chapter, I outlined how hiring works and why college graduates struggle to land their first job. But those who finally break through quickly encounter a second harsh reality.

College students expect to make $103,880 after graduation – almost twice the reality

 **Wyatte Grantham-Philips**
USA TODAY

Published 1:46 p.m. ET May 5, 2022 | Updated 3:05 p.m. ET May 7, 2022

Figure 18. College graduates hold unrealistic expectations about how much money they will make.

(Source: Wyatte Grantham-Philips, "College Students Expect to Make $103,880 after Graduation—Almost Twice the Reality," *USA Today*, February 5, 2022.)

Their expected financial success does not materialize. In my conversations with young adults, disillusionment and frustration have set in based on a simple formula I have discussed often with our daughters.

Happiness = Reality - Expectations.

Human beings tend to find happiness when the reality they experience meets or exceeds their expectations about what their reality would be. When your expectations are grand, you must facilitate a top-end reality to feel accomplished and fulfilled. And this is why I've always had three huge issues with the path.

First, as highlighted in the study shown in Figure 18 and many others, teenagers become college graduates with insanely high expectations. As a result, from day one, they tend to chase their high expectations frantically rather than enjoying life in a calm state of mind. Second, the massive investment the path requires sits in the "gut" of young adults. As months and years pass without the promised reality materializing, the burden of "what I and/or others invested" weighs them down with guilt. And, last, there are so many activities, tests, projects, homework, and practices that teenagers are constantly stressed out and tired. There is no time or guidance to teach a teenager how to become a young adult with the confidence, mindset, and tools to create happiness from the inside out.

Think about it. How much time is proactively allocated—with lots of guidance and thought leadership—to help your teenager explore "What makes me happy?" Not what makes parents or friends or teachers happy, but what makes them happy from the inside out? Very little, right?

Not surprisingly, many teenagers become young adults who, despite dedicating most of their lives to fulfilling the perceived requirements for economic success, cross the finish line and find their reality falls far short of their expectations. The disorientation of uncertainty now replaces the comfort of certainty. Rule following and task completion are no longer rewarded. And, for many, the career they chose as a teenager is (shockingly) different from what they now wish they could do for forty-plus hours a week. In a real-world example, I recently sat down with a twentysomething friend of Brooke's and heard this verbatim. We talked for forty-five minutes, so I'm paraphrasing her feedback.

I started by asking about her career, why she chose it, and how things were going. She said, "I picked my career [nursing] at sixteen when I was a different person than I am today. Yes, I like parts of my job, and I make good money, which is one of the main reasons I picked it. But I'm increasingly unsure if this is what I want to do. I'm worried I made a big mistake."

I asked if she was unhappy enough to consider shutting it down and pivoting to something else. She said, "I do think about that a lot, but honestly, I have no idea what I would do. I don't have the financial security to quit my job and go several weeks or months without income. And, even if I did, how do I figure out a new career? I'd have to go back to school and start in some kind of entry-level position making much less than I do now. I don't know, it just seems like I'm stuck with this."

Finally, I asked if her sunk costs felt like a burden. She said, "Yes, in a huge way. I pretty much hated college because I had to study constantly. I feel like I missed out on the college experience. The money, time, and stress I invested are too overwhelming just to walk away. I would feel like it was all for nothing."

Again, that is a microcosm of a longer conversation, but I hear these sentiments often. Many young adults feel paralyzed by the chasm between their disconcerting reality and unreasonably high expectations because they aren't prepared for such a scenario. They're uncomfortable navigating uncertainty. They believe credentials are necessary to start something new. They have invested far too much to give up. They spent so much time doing what they were told that they now lack the confidence to pivot of their own volition. And, in their haze of confusion, frustration, and unhappiness, what do they hear from the adults who failed to prepare them adequately? Dismissive criticism that they can't handle the demands of the real world.

What a bunch of snowflakes! Almost half of recent college graduates are not 'emotionally' prepared for a 9-5, damning survey finds

- **A bombshell survey has revealed that huge numbers of young professionals are emotionally unprepared to survive the modern workday**
- **A majority of workers aged 22-28 feel burnt out every week, and 51 percent have sought help for their mental health in the last year**
- **Large numbers of those surveyed slated colleges for failing to prepare them for their careers**

By WILL POTTER FOR DAILYMAIL.COM
PUBLISHED: 14:13 EST, 15 February 2023 | **UPDATED:** 18:19 EST, 15 February 2023

Figure 19. Today's young adults are constantly attacked and diminished by the generation that raised them.

(Source: Will Potter, "What a Bunch of Snowflakes! Almost Half of Recent College Graduates Are Not 'Emotionally' Prepared for a 9-5," *DailyMail*, February 15, 2023.)

It would be funny if it weren't so anger-inducing (at least, it is for me).

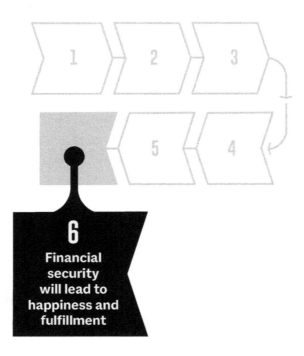

And there you have it, the foolproof way for teenagers to uniquely find success, happiness, and fulfillment based on a formulaic and linear path. Now that we've walked through every element, it makes perfect sense! Sorry, I thought I'd throw in a little sarcasm.

In all seriousness, while I do not expect you to agree with everything I say, I hope you're at least evaluating what you chose to believe up until now. Have you previously considered when school was created and why? Do you have a new point of view about what school is designed to deliver? Did you gain a new appreciation for the immense pressure your teenager endures? Are you not just open to but even intrigued by options other than college? Were you surprised by how college graduates struggle to get jobs, much less enjoy success, happiness, and fulfillment?

I hope so because the rest of this book will focus on converting your new point of view and curiosity into actionable steps as you and your teenager set out on a new journey. If the path represents our villain, our superhero is a growth mindset.

It's time to don your cape.

"Good choices are like compounding interest—over time, they stack together and lead to lots of goodness. And the opposite is true as well."

SECTION 4

GROWTH MINDSET

In 2011, I read *Mindset: The New Psychology of Success* by Carol Dweck, which will always be on my list of top ten recommended books. I will use many of its core components to guide you in developing the mindset necessary to be confident about not following the path. Why? Because mainstream society will come at you with ferocity and vigor. I heard it more times than I could count—"I can't help but think you're setting your child up for failure."

Nah. Hold my beer.

CHAPTER 15

Growth versus Fixed Mindset

Fixed Mindset	Growth Mindset
Intelligence is static	Intelligence can be developed
Desire to look smart	Desire to learn
Avoid challenges; stay in my lane	Embrace challenges; be bold
Give up easily; get upset by mistakes	Persist in the face of setbacks; mistakes welcome
See effort as fruitless or worse	See effort as the path to mastery
Tend to ignore useful feedback	Criticism is how I get better
Feel threatened by the success of others	Find lessons and inspiration in the success of others
I can't do it	I can't do it *yet*
Result: Tends to plateau early and settle	**Result:** Reaches ever-higher levels of achievement

The rest of this section delves into a growth mindset and how to build it in you and your teenager.[3] Before we get to the growth mindset, let's focus on the fixed mindset that will, with absolute certainty, prevent you or your teenager from having any success with what I propose. You must "know it when you see it" to eliminate a fixed mindset. And I mean that—do not let a fixed mindset or any elements of it exist in you or your teenager because it will eat you up.

There are three prime examples, fostered by the path, of how a fixed mindset becomes entrenched in a teenager (which is extremely hard to change later): (1) looking smart, (2) avoiding risk, and (3) needing external reassurance.

LOOKING SMART

Grades represent the tangible measurement system used to drive compliance and evoke fear. Kids learn early on that:

- A = people view me as smart and high achieving.
- C = people view me as average and unlikely to "reach my potential."
- F = people view me as dumb and likely to be a failure.

Being viewed as smart and high achieving feels good, which motivates teenagers to do whatever it takes to make As. If you spend time in a high school classroom, you will repeatedly hear the same question asked—"Will this be on the test?" If the answer is yes, teenagers will commit to temporarily learning, memorizing, or cheating their way to an A to maintain or reach "smart" status. If the answer is no, they will not care and move on. But it's not just the teenagers.

---

3 "Growth Mindset Toolkit," Transforming Education, accessed February 5, 2024, https://transformingeducation.org/resources/growth-mindset-toolkit/.

Socially conscious parents care deeply about being viewed as having smart kids who get accepted by a "good" college. As a result, they go above and beyond to fill in the gaps—energy, stress, anxiety, cajoling, teacher conferences, helping with homework, doing projects at 1:00 a.m., and filling out applications. Their teenager, not surprisingly, becomes a young adult lacking the confidence, fortitude, and tool set to do hard things on their own and becomes highly sensitive when called out.

AVOIDING RISK

Let me pose a few questions. How mentally tough and self-confident is your teenager? If suddenly put into a new or difficult situation, how effectively does she settle in and calmly work her way through it? How well does he manage conflict on his own? What percentage of their time is dedicated to new ventures—of their own volition—with an unknown risk/reward outcome?

The answers are far from ideal for most teenagers I have encountered over the last decade. They are often mentally fragile, terrible at conflict management, do not handle difficult situations well, and lack the self-confidence to try anything if the outcome isn't known. Looking smart is so ingrained that they seek to maintain it at all costs. As a result, they minimize uncertainty, avoid risks or new challenges, and do what they're told (no conflict, please), which is the very definition of a fixed mindset.

EXTERNAL REASSURANCE

Over the last ten to fifteen years, an increasingly common refrain has been that today's young adults constantly need reassurance and recognition. You hear it all the time—"Nothing seems to satisfy them. They're so entitled!" I try not to blame young adults for this because most of them are raised on the path. While I am not a clinical psychologist, I believe three elements have caused (or, at least, have contributed heavily to) their need for external reassurance.

First, the rise of social media—emphasizing the perfect online persona to get the most "likes" intensifies a fixed-mindset tendency to feel threatened by others' achievements. There are countless studies and research on this, so feel free to draw your own conclusions. However, I have become convinced it matters.

Second, the amplification of pursuing high achievement results in a near-constant cacophony of "Way to go!" or "I think you're smart" feedback loops. It's as if teenagers evolve into pets, doing whatever it takes to get a treat for doing what they're told. When the treats stop, disillusionment sets in.

Third, by the time they're young adults, so much has been invested that they constantly compare themselves to their peers, feel like they're coming up short, and need external reassurance. I observe this in many young adults who are frustrated that their happiness equation (Happiness = Reality - Expectations) feels upside down. Their reality falls far short of expectations, and they don't want to hear criticism; they want validation that it was all worth it.

Don't allow it—any of it.

CHAPTER 16

Play the Long Game

As a parent, you feel tremendous social pressure to "present" a high-achieving teenager. Social media is a rolling feed of "We're so proud of ____ for ____." We're all guilty of it to varying degrees because our child reflects our ability to be a good parent. And, of course, it's okay to celebrate your child's achievements!

That said, remember how I opened this book. Based on what is celebrated and recognized during the teenage years, our daughters achieved nothing in high school. They walked across the graduation stage with no colored tassels on their caps nor pins on their gowns. And, as I said, it was all by design.

We were playing the long game.

We were not trying to raise high-achieving fifteen-year-olds; everything we did was focused on enabling high-achieving twenty-five-year-olds. That was our philosophy, and we discussed it often among ourselves and even turned it into a running joke with our teenage daughters about how people probably thought they were losers. We had to become comfortable and confident in this mindset and repeatedly remind our daughters of it through conversations like these:

[Regarding academic performance]

When you're twenty-five, you're no longer appraised on the ability to retain and regurgitate information on a test. Once you leave school, that requirement rarely exists. Don't worry about having a lower GPA than your friends. Instead of studying extra hours to make an A on a test, you're learning emotional intelligence and how to crush an interview. Those things don't matter much now, but they will later.

[Regarding rule following]

Kicking ass and taking names when you're twenty-five isn't about following orders; it's about being bold, taking calculated risks, and learning from each experience. Don't worry about needing a minimum of 1,000 words in your paper. It's a dumb rule. Provide a "solution" that isn't preordained, is of your own design, and is highly compelling. And keep practicing because the confidence to repeatedly do so will serve you well later.

[Regarding consequences]

Feeling accomplished and fulfilled at twenty-five is rarely driven by waiting for or expecting someone else to do things for you. If you wait until the last minute and cannot finish your project on time, we're not helping you. It is your problem, consequences, and learning opportunity. The only way you'll learn to be independent is to be allowed to be independent.

We held many conversations like these throughout our daughters' teenage years, on various topics, and slowly but surely they got it. I won't say they didn't care what other people thought about them—we all care. But I do know that now—at twenty-three and twenty-six—they are self-motivated, not afraid to take risks, and can get things done without needing to be reminded.

We live in a media-obsessed world where we're coerced to fixate on current events and breaking news. We seek instant information, reactions, recognition, and punishment. Everything is about the here and now. Do not fall into that trap with your teenager. Your mindset must be to tune out what everyone else values, rewards, recognizes, and punishes so that you and your teenager can take a different and better approach.

You're playing the long game.

CHAPTER 17

Grades Don't Matter

Earlier, I discussed why pursuing good grades is increasingly irrelevant, but now, let's be bold. The "get good grades" mindset is so entrenched that you cannot be indecisive with your teenager. Let them know and repeatedly remind them that grades in school don't matter.

The New York Times

What Straight-A Students Get Wrong

If you always succeed in school, you're not setting yourself up for success in life.

By Adam Grant
Dr. Grant is an organizational psychologist and a contributing opinion writer.

Dec. 8, 2018

Figure 20. A fantastic article about how and why academic excellence is not a strong predictor of career excellence.

(Source: Adam Grant, "What Straight-A Students Get Wrong," *The New York Times*, December 8, 2018.)

I know, I know. That is an inflammatory statement for many and the opposite of what most parents believe and enforce. But, before you cast me out as being hyperradical or clueless, let's build on Seth Godin's manifesto and leave no stone unturned when evaluating the specifics of what school is.

Our society has decided there's nothing more important than getting your education. Have you ever looked up the definition of the word education? It is defined as "the process of receiving or giving systematic instruction, especially at a school or university." The important word is "systematic." That is what school always felt like and what I observed in my daughters and their friends. Systematic means "done or acting according to a fixed plan or system; methodical." So, when you pressure your teenager to get good grades, you're instructing them to be proficient at *receiving instruction in a fixed, methodical way.* My wife and I saw little to no value in such proficiency.

If you're ready to explore this subject matter with your teenager, start with a conversation in which you explain precisely how the education system works.

In our country, school is required by law. Until age sixteen, you must receive instruction and conform to the rules. The adults are in charge, and there will be consequences if you misbehave.

Everyone starts at a specific age and is processed in the same order. You are expected to keep up as your peer (age) group advances one grade at a time. If you can't keep up the pace and perform at the necessary standards, you will be told something is wrong with you. If that happens, tests will determine why you can't keep up and accommodations will be made for someone "like you."

For example, you might be told you must repeat a grade, be given medication, be shifted to less demanding courses, and/or be given more time to complete assignments. The system isn't the issue—you are. Those in charge will tell you they're not trying to make you feel dumb or inadequate. They must maintain the pace for the greater good and can't let you hold back those who keep up without special accommodations.

Each semester or grading period, you must learn the information the system deems necessary at your age. You have no say in how that information is delivered. You will read the same textbooks, hear the same lectures, and be assigned the same homework.

You will be regularly assessed on your ability to absorb, process, memorize, and regurgitate instruction. You must complete quizzes, tests, and projects in the same amount of time as everyone else. You are rated using a numerical grading system applied to all activities, for all participants.

You will be recognized, celebrated, and told you're smart if you consistently achieve high grades. If you cannot consistently achieve high grades, you will be told to accept you have limitations and can only amount to so much. Again, the system is not the problem—if you cannot conform and excel, you are the problem.

Let's not kid ourselves. It's not as if the education system is a mystery. What purpose is served by hiding its inner workings from your teenager?

School has benefits, especially at a young age, as this is when children learn the basics of reading, writing, and arithmetic. And most teachers, administrators, and counselors within the education system mean well. I do not seek to denigrate them. But, designed over 150 years ago to serve an increasingly irrelevant purpose today, the education system is bloated, antiquated, and ineffective. In most ways, it is a glorified babysitting service kids are sent to while their parents work, and insisting its participants mindlessly seek rewards within it leads to a fixed mindset and lack of curiosity. Still, teenagers are relentlessly told, "Nothing is more important than getting your education!" Can we please stop?

As I said at the start of this chapter, I challenge you to embrace boldness and a new mindset, then share it with your teenager. Instead of prioritizing academic achievement, encourage them to become a thriving young adult able to continuously, deftly, and confidently self-direct their learning. Start (as early as possible in middle school) by sending your teenager links to online articles that broaden their perspective and open their minds to a new world where they're no longer forced to comply mindlessly.

Psychology Today: Inverse Relationship Between Grades and Innovation

"Ironically and tragically, rather than adapt our educational system to the needs of our modern times we have doubled down on the old system, so it is harder today than ever before for young people to retain and build upon their natural curiosity and creativity."
– Peter Gray Ph.D.

Figure 21. Peter Gray is one of many psychologists who believe the education system is obsolete.

(Source: Peter Gray, "Inverse Relationship between GPA and Innovative Orientation," *Psychology Today*, April 30, 2016.)

Then, hold conversations in which you instill the confidence to not participate in the rat race and suggest new outcomes to pursue with vigor.

The pressure about grades is never-ending. You will feel intense pressure to conform, and most of your friends will hate school largely due to this pressure.

That isn't how we'll roll. The grades you attain in school are entirely up to you. We will not pressure or pay you to get good grades and will rarely celebrate a test score or good grade. Why? Three reasons.

First, most subjects you are forced to "learn" will not be interesting or relevant to you. If a subject is interesting or relevant, there will be limited options to apply what you're being taught. Thus, pursuing good grades is essentially fool's gold because you retain very little of what you supposedly learn by the time you can fully apply it. We prefer you focus your time and energy on discovering, learning, and applying relevant information of your own choosing.

Second, the whole point of a grading system is to force you to learn and give rewards when you do so (if there were no grades, you would be free to choose what you learn, right?). We cannot think of a valid reason to implore you to excel in this system because, once you finish school, it will only be your reality again if you choose to reenter it. We prefer you focus on what will be rewarded for the rest of your life—an innate drive to self-direct your learning.

Third, in addition to being told you're smart, getting good grades in high school is primarily about getting into a "good" college. We don't care if you even go to college (much less a "good" one). We'll return to that conversation later, but do not strive for good grades to become suitable for something later.

Last, because school is compulsory and some classes are mandatory, you need to pass those classes. Your job is to get through a system you're required to participate in, and our job is to ensure you take away very little of what it tells you to prioritize.

Once you and your teenager lean into this approach—you guessed it—grades won't matter. Instead, your teenager will adopt a self-directed approach to learning, which is critical for a growth mindset.

CHAPTER 18

Averages Do Not Apply to Individuals

Teenagers and parents are inundated with information and research promoting the importance of a college degree. Simultaneously, most information creates fear about the downside of not getting a degree. Regardless of the source, all of it is based on one thing—averages. I've read hundreds of reports and studies and always noticed:

- The terminology is mostly passive, such as "it can be" or "you should have."
- Conclusions use terms like "on average," "more likely to," or "has been shown to."
- The stronger the position for "get your education" and "college is invaluable," the more likely a college or education-centric organization did the study/research.

Why? Because a college or university guarantees nothing. If you attend and graduate, you're not guaranteed a job, minimum salary, or seed money. Instead, the statements and conclusions regarding the return on investment of a college degree fall back to the law of averages:

- The average college graduate's annual salary is "x" percent higher than nongraduates.
- On average, college graduates are "x" percent more likely to land higher-paying jobs than nongraduates.

- College graduates are "x" percent less likely to be unemployed than nongraduates.
- College graduates can see through walls and melt carbon with their eyes.

I may have made the last one up, but you get the point. The message is clear—if you stray from the path, you will ruin your kid's future by significantly lowering their earnings ceiling and introducing increased risk of unemployment. There is one core flaw in that message.

Averages do not apply to individuals. Never have.

Each of us is born a unique individual with our own DNA strands. Each of us is then raised in a unique environment and time in history. Each of us interacts with thousands of people, many of whom say or do things that uniquely impact our mindset, self-confidence, and knowledge. Each of us has countless experiences that leave unique impressions on us. As a result, none of us are accurately represented by any average. If you feel otherwise, you have a fixed mindset.

I suggest you share with your teenager multiple studies, articles, or blog posts that conclude things like, "On average, college graduates are ____ percent more likely to achieve ____ compared to noncollege graduates." If left to their own devices, they will conclude the data and research are clear and that they need a college degree to get ahead in life. But they're not left to their own devices; they have you. Help them form a more dynamic and vibrant mindset through a conversation like this:

It's essential to remember there is no such thing as an average representing you as an individual. As a result, this study's "average" noncollege graduate has almost nothing in common with you.

The "average" noncollege graduate did not dedicate their teenage years to building a growth mindset and a feature-rich tool belt of highly valued, real-world skills. You are and will.

The "average" noncollege graduate did not proactively use their time outside of the classroom preparing and building self-confidence to kick ass as a young adult. You are and will.

The "average" noncollege graduate did not invest deeply in building emotional intelligence and conversational skills. You are and will.

And, on top of that, none of those noncollege graduates possess your unique combination of DNA, self-driven knowledge, and robust support system.

Going through life attempting to meet or exceed averages is the essence of a fixed mindset. Ignore this study and every other one like it.

One last thing: while the income gap between individuals with and without college degrees is statistically well-documented, I am convinced there is a simple "why" behind the data.

Noncollege graduates give up.

Overwhelmed by the "averages" and declarative statements that a college degree is *required* for good jobs, they choose not to pursue them. They stay in their lane by accepting the mainstream point of view as gospel and settling for lower-paying jobs they believe they're eligible for. I already shared how Lauren—confident, prepared, and empowered after her teen years—debunked the mainstream mindset. In the last three chapters, I'll go through exactly how she did it—step-by-step.

Please don't allow yourself or your teenager to form a fixed mindset through which effort investments are based on the average outcomes of large groups of people. Empower your teenager with a growth mindset to view effort as the path to mastery and, perhaps most importantly, to find lessons and inspiration in the success of individuals, not group averages.

CHAPTER 19

Embrace Uncertainty

Human beings crave certainty. Believing you can lay out a plan, follow it, and get what you expect results in a sense of control. And, of course, sometimes we are in control. We put our minds to something important to us and make it happen. I value and respect situations where someone makes something happen through relentless pursuit and hard work. That said, for me, the certainty train left the station for good the moment I was told Lauren had stage 3 cancer.

As shared in the first section, I decided years before that the world was unpredictable and would increasingly be so, but that moment sealed it. I sent the following texts a few hours after her diagnosis.

To my precious daughter. I'm as shocked and sad and angry as I've ever been. No human being deserves to hear the words "you've got cancer" but today you heard that. My 20-year-old daughter heard that.

But now that you heard those words and know them to be your reality, the only thing that matters is facing it. And we're gonna face the f-ck out of this.

I will be with you at every step. If you don't understand something, tell me and I will learn it for you. If you aren't sure what to do next, tell me and I will find out. If you're feeling sad or down, tell me and I'll make you laugh. If you need a shoulder to cry on, I've got two of them. If you need to scream at someone, scream at me and I'll take every word of it.

I'm not going to promise you everything will be ok because I don't know what's going to happen. Empty promises serve no purpose and we're not going to waste our time on shit like that.

What I will promise you is we will face this together every minute of every day and there is nothing—absolutely nothing—that you will need that I will not make sure you get. I'm your rock and I will be immovable.

Let's kick some cancer ass.

I've reread that text many times and always get emotional. But what I hope resonates most is my confession that I didn't know what would happen or if everything would be okay. Embracing uncertainty was a recurring theme in conversations with our daughters. The goal was a mindset to accept uncertainty and even thrive within it. During Lauren's most challenging moment, I needed to walk the walk.

With that in mind, here's the deal. If your mindset is to manufacture your child's future reality many years from now (such as making the NBA, becoming a doctor, or being a millionaire), please stop. That is the mindset the path espouses—an if/then/else formula to present the illusion of certainty. That cannot be your mindset. You must become comfortable with and accept that uncertainty is the only sure thing. Once you do that, you must walk the walk. But how?

> I had to go from feeling no motivation, no direction, just simply "existing" to finding what makes me want to get out of bed every day feeling motivated and then go to sleep feeling accomplished.

As I'll detail in the final section, Brooke was directionless and unhappy after dropping out of college. The long journey to finding herself started with a simple first step—"get out of bed every day feeling motivated and then go to sleep feeling accomplished." I know it sounds oversimplified, but this is the mindset you will observe when talking with an intrinsically happy and fulfilled person.

Someone innately comfortable in their own skin does not go through life trying to live up to the expectations of others. Instead, they learn and prioritize what causes happiness in the present and schedule their daily activities accordingly. As we get older and pick up responsibilities (spouse, mortgage, kids, etc.), this gets much harder to do, which is why we helped our daughters adopt this mindset in their teenage years and early adulthood. It is a core building block to a strong growth mindset enabling long-term fulfillment and happiness.

You can engage your teenager in a conversation like this.

Your future is unknown and cannot be predicted. To which I'm sure you will respond, "Yeah, I know," but it's important that we dwell on this. When you're young, with limited life experience, you tend to build a plan you believe you can execute. If I do x, I will get y, leading to z.

That absolutely can happen. But it almost always does not. Does that mean you set no goals for the future or set no milestones you want to achieve? Definitely not.

If you want to set a goal for later today, next week, or two years from now . . . go for it! Set your goal and pursue it, but do so with the expectation that uncertainty will show up at some point. Something you couldn't have predicted might cause you not to achieve your goal. By the time you achieve your goal, something might have happened such that attaining it doesn't feel like you thought it would.

Expect uncertainty and become comfortable and confident leaning into it. Because doing so will set you apart.

Help your teenager become comfortable prioritizing and being thankful for their present, which takes practice. Once they become comfortable prioritizing the present, help them narrow down their activities on a day-to-day basis. Help them eliminate stress over "what if" scenarios and the endless possibilities of what could happen. The reality is they (and you) don't know. I will always feel that conversations like these led to Lauren's TED Talk comment the day she was told she had stage 3 cancer.

CHAPTER 20

Rethink Risk

Many parents attempt to micromanage virtually every aspect of their teenager's life. The commonly used term is helicopter parenting.

A Psychologist Calls Out The Many Dangers Of Helicopter Parenting

Mark Travers Contributor ⓘ
I write about the world of psychology.

Figure 22. Helicopter parents engineer safety in the short term with consequences in the long term.

(Source: Mark Travers, "A Psychologist Calls Out the Many Dangers of Helicopter Parenting," *Forbes*, November 22, 2022. https://www.forbes.com/sites/traversmark/2022/11/30/a-psychologist-calls-out-the-many-dangers-of-helicopter-parenting/?sh=8d149e320d04)

Unfortunately, these parents tend to raise teenagers who become timid, overly cautious young adults scared of risk. If this resembles or describes you, I hope you will consider an adjustment.

Earlier, I mentioned how I enjoy listening to company founders talk about the risks they took as they tried to transition from an idea to a fledgling business with revenue generation. For some, the early risks were minor, bite-sized chunks. But, for others, the early risks were all-or-nothing in nature. Regardless, a constant takeaway when listening to this podcast is "no risk it, no biscuit" (mainly because I really like biscuits, especially with sausage gravy).

Successful people excel at decision-making. Every decision you make is a bet, and a bet entails risk. What sets successful people apart is they outperform others at calculated risk-taking. Said differently, they consistently make good bets (i.e., decisions) by carefully selecting situations where they invest the least amount to achieve consistently positive outcomes. It is a critical enabler of a growth mindset.

How do you enable your teenager to excel at calculated risk-taking? What will not work is preventing your teenager from taking any risks or "helicoptering in" when anything starts to feel risky. Instead, start with the basics and work your way into it.

To begin, explain to your teenager there are three costs with any risk or bet:

1. **Hard costs**: Money and assets.
2. **Soft costs**: Your mental well-being, stress, relationship impact, anxiety, etc.
3. **Time**: Arguably your most precious asset.

Plus a fourth significant cost most people don't consider but the best risk-takers master.

4. **Opportunity costs**: What you could do, instead, with all three of the above.

Everything you choose to do in life has a risk/reward spectrum. For example, let's say you set up a lemonade stand on a Saturday, and no one shows up for four hours:

1. **Hard costs:** Meager, a few bucks.
2. **Soft costs:** You might feel disappointed or sad your table "failed."
3. **Time:** Five hours to set up, break down, and sit behind the table.
4. **Opportunity cost:** Fun with your friends at the pool.

Setting up a lemonade stand is a low-investment/low-outcome bet. And, even if it flops, you'll learn that your neighborhood might not be a good place to sell lemonade. Next time you invest a few hours to make a few bucks, you will try something different. *This* is how you learn to take risks responsibly. In the next section I'll provide several examples, but for now, work on your teenager's risk mindset in three ways.

First, most people equate risk with danger. When you take risks, bad things can happen. Yes, that is one way to think about risk, and there are situations and decisions where risk is hazardous. Help your teenager think about risk differently regarding happiness and fulfillment.

Every decision you make is a bet. And every bet—even setting up a lemonade stand—has some risk. Instead of viewing risk as scary, we encourage you to think of risk as simply the act of doing something without knowing the outcome. Might the outcome not be what you hoped or expected? Yep, it might.

So, start small and learn from the outcome. Then go a bit bigger. Then go even bigger. Over time, you will build confidence that risk isn't scary; it is how you achieve and learn from outcomes.

As an aside—this is why college is a poor representation of the mindset you're building. There is no option to "start small"; instead, you must invest massive amounts of time, energy, stress, anxiety, and money before you experience any outcome. Even worse, there is no guaranteed outcome. In a casino, you can place a bet on a team to win a game and know exactly what you will win or lose based on the outcome. College doesn't work that way. The upfront cost is enormous, and the outcome is unknown.

Second, evaluate how much mainstream media your teenager consumes and have a conversation as follows.

Media has always operated via a repeatable and highly profitable formula. Find the wildest exceptions + present them as norms + scare people = profits.

It appeals to our most banal instincts, and we have difficulty ignoring it. If you cannot ignore it, you must, at a minimum, not take any of it at face value. If you fall victim to their formula, you will view the world as full of danger, traps, and bad people. And that mindset will highly influence your decision-making and cause you to be risk averse. It will paralyze you.

Third, introduce the critical importance of opportunity cost and help your teenager understand how to evaluate what they invest versus what they could invest instead. I'll share specific examples in the next section, but the conversation can start like this for now.

Because we chose not to follow the path, you are empowered (with our guidance). For example, instead of studying for hours memorizing information you don't care about to get an A on a test, you get to spend that time differently.

You get to learn how to evaluate trade-offs and opportunity costs by doing things you feel motivated and excited to do. As you do them, you will attain various outcomes and learn how to assess what you invested, what you could have invested instead, and what different outcomes you hope to achieve.

Things get complicated when you're an adult, which is why your teenage years are the best time to build this muscle memory. You have few responsibilities and are taking on low risk. Building this skill set early enables you to master it sooner—and that will make you a great decision-maker.

For most teenagers, these conversations change everything.

CHAPTER 21

Unlimited Potential

When you implement everything in this section, your teenager has a vibrant growth mindset that makes a human being damn near unstoppable.

They understand future happiness and fulfillment aren't tied to adolescent achievements, nor can they be scheduled for the future like a calendar invite. Instead, they know it's an inside-out, self-driven process that requires constant care and feeding.

They do not need to be proficient at receiving instruction in a fixed way or system. Grades don't matter, allowing them to exhale and release the pressure of trying to look smart. They now know there is no wrong answer when the voice in their head asks, "What do I want to learn today?"

They are not defined by averages. Instead, they're intrigued by and ready to poke and prod at their individual traits. Who am I? What am I naturally good at? What causes me to feel sad or happy? What causes the voice in my head to pat me on the back? Rather than wasting time with worthless information they don't care about, they get to explore and turn over rocks.

They do not allow external media and fearmongering voices to impact their mindset negatively. They refuse to be manipulated and will ignore the mindless drivel, assume command of their present, and be ever curious about the future.

Looking ahead, they now accept the future is unknown and there is no perfect plan. They will appreciate waking up each day, knowing that a day can come in various flavors. Some will be terrible, and some will be wonderful. Some will be disappointing, and some will be uplifting. Some days, nothing of any consequence will happen, while others will represent a monumental breakthrough. Some take you one step closer to achieving a goal, and some eviscerate your desire to pursue a goal. Such is life. Throw your hands up and enjoy the ride.

Possessing a new risk mindset and no longer paralyzed by fear, they will burst at the seams to try new things. They will not worry about hiding their mistakes or developing a good lie because they're encouraged to make and learn from mistakes. Lots of them.

As their parent, you get to engage and bond with your teenager in a new way.

Being a teenager is hard enough. You no longer need to pretend to be happy, smart, motivated, or perfect. Our primary demands are to be a good person, build a growth mindset, and develop high emotional intelligence.

Beyond that, you get to explore, be empowered, make choices, and hold yourself accountable to your expectations. You get to be openly mad and sad and confused and angry. You can make mistakes, face the consequences, and decide whether to repeat the same error.

What a liberating mindset!

Now we're ready to rock. Anything is possible. Your teenager feels like their potential is, and always will be, *unlimited*. So, what do you do with this awesome mindset and new bundle of energy? How do you channel and focus it?

Let's get into it.

"It's okay to stop doing what everyone else tells you and, instead, own your story and build confidence by doing what you want. When you take that approach, a beautiful pattern takes shape. One thing leads to another."

SECTION 5

THRIVE

Another quote from Seth Godin (sorry, I think he's smart).[4]

> *Once we see that we're able to own our story, we gain a huge amount of power. And we retain that power for as long as we refuse to hand it over to someone else.*

I *love* that mindset. Own your story, be empowered, and retain it at all costs. That, above all else, is what your teenager's new journey is about. My wife and I disagreed with the path's rules, fear-based approach, and false promises. In this fifth and final section, you'll learn what we did and how you can engage and empower your teenager to thrive through new conversations you start today.

---

4 Seth Godin, "Blaming the Weather Is a Trap," *Seth's Blog,* December 15, 2021, https://seths.blog/2021/12/blaming-the-weather-is-a-trap/.

CHAPTER 22

New versus Old

If the path is linear, formulaic, and unnecessary, your new approach is fluid, unconventional, and vital. No longer are you and your teen traipsing down a one-way path with a series of sequential steps. Instead, you will engage each other through new conversations focused on empowering your teenager to continuously, deftly, and confidently self-direct their never-ending development. Within that long-term goal, three words drove our approach to empower our daughters.

The word thrive means to grow or develop well or vigorously. I cannot think of a better way to describe what we hoped to see in a young adult charting their own course and experiencing life in a completely new way (once they lived independently). You are constantly growing and developing. You never become stagnant.

The word deft means neatly skillful and quick in one's movement. We did not want our daughters to correlate learning with how school delivers it—receiving instruction in a fixed way or system. We wanted them to be uniquely able to find new things to learn and easily pivot if needed (with any aspect of their life). When anything comes up that requires you to know something new, you are quick in movement. You never get stuck.

Last is confidence, which means the feeling or belief that one can rely on someone or something. For our daughters, we always wanted the "someone" in that definition to be the voice in their heads. Yes, you will have friends, partners, and family members you rely on, but your ability to thrive will always start with having firm trust in yourself. Building that necessary level of belief takes time, focused energy, and experience in doing so.

With those goals in mind, below are the core topics for your new conversations.

In summary, on the path, your teenager follows the rules, does what they're told, pursues good grades, excels at completing tasks assigned by others, and picks a career they'll do for decades. Going forward, your teen will stop taking things so seriously, self-direct their development, build critical skills that school ignores, and become a thriving and in-high-demand young adult who never feels stuck.

CHAPTER 23

Embrace Freedom

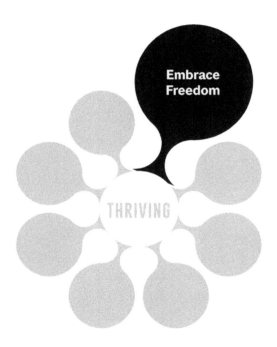

Trust me, I know firsthand that raising teenagers is challenging. No matter how many things you get right, mistakes will often be made. And no matter how strong your relationship is with your teenager, there will be times when you can't stand each other. At the same time, I mentioned earlier how hard it is to be a teenager without external pressure. Our teenage daughters were sad, angry, aloof, confused, or disengaged on more occasions than I could ever count. It isn't all peaches and cream.

That said, it is critically important to remember that your teenager is a little kid in a grown-up body. Unfortunately, on the path, these "little kids" are pressured to act like adults who need to study hard, pursue excellence, build a strong work ethic, and be responsible, which doesn't leave much time to . . . be a kid. These are all good traits to develop, of course, but most adults in a teenager's life take things too seriously and apply too much pressure. I often find myself thinking, "Geez, ease up."

I strongly encourage you to do exactly that—ease up. Or, if necessary, insist that your teenager ease up. Give a lot of freedom to be a kid while holding them accountable for developing a few core traits that form a strong foundation.

Everyone knows a jerk when they meet one, and we will not allow you to be that. You will be a kind and respectful human being— that is nonnegotiable.

Do not lie or hide things from us. There is no need. We expect you to make many mistakes and wrong decisions—it's okay. We're not interested in punishing you. We're interested in helping you learn through guidance and experiences. Go do stuff.

Don't try to make us or anyone else proud of you. Instead, focus on making you proud of yourself (the voice in your head will tell you how you're doing). There might not be a better habit than this to develop, and we hope you work on it. A lot.

You don't need to "Fake it till you make it" or pretend to have it all together. You're supposed to be a bit of a hot mess right now—it's okay. Sit down with us anytime you feel things are spinning out of control, and we'll do our best to help. Again, our goal will never be to punish or judge.

Being popular or anointed as a teenager means nothing (I know, it feels like it means everything). The more time and energy you invest trying to get other people to like you, the more miserable you will become. First and foremost: like yourself. If you ever need suggestions about what to like about yourself, we have lots of them.

We will not taskmaster you because doing so is a disservice to your development. You are (mostly) in charge of what you choose to do or not do. Our goal is to help you become a confident decision-maker, which means we must allow you to make decisions (to a point). Instead of implementing rules you must follow, we will provide a lot of freedom and add rules when necessary.

Boiling it down to the absolute basics, we did our best to emphasize four things throughout their teenage years: (1) be a good person, (2) be honest, (3) like yourself, and (4) learn to make good decisions. Beyond those four things, there were very few rules (for example, neither of them ever had a curfew, and we never checked their phones).

We mostly let them do their thing until they stepped over the line (which absolutely happened), at which point we discussed what happened. Punishments were handed out here and there, but mostly, we approached those situations with a "learn from your mistake" approach versus a "be punished for your mistake" verdict.

We empowered them with freedom while insisting on open dialogue and firmly establishing final decision-making authority when necessary.

We will start with lots of freedom and a few important rules. With great freedom comes great responsibility, and your responsibility is that you must talk with us often. The less we speak, the more rules will be implemented. The more we talk, the fewer the rules.

Why must you talk to us? Think back to two years ago. Can you picture yourself at that age? Okay, now, how much have you learned since then? Are you more knowledgeable and mature? Could you offer some good advice to yourself two years ago?

Right. Well, that doesn't stop. You'll feel the same way two years from now when thinking about who you are today. And again, two years from that. And we, your parents, have accumulated thirty years of life experience you do not yet have. Just like you could help that person you were two years ago, we can help you.

Again, open communication means mostly freedom, but sometimes we will act with final decision-making authority and impose our will in a way you disagree with. We assure you that those times will be few and far between. If you go against our will with those decisions, there will be severe consequences for you, and rules will be added.

This often elicits two immediate reactions from parents.

First, I often hear, "That's crazy; you can't give a teenager that kind of freedom. They need discipline and structure. Their brains are developing, and they cannot be trusted to make decisions. You must keep them safe from themselves." I understand there are many trains of thought on this and no guaranteed correct answer. Many parents believe an approach like ours results in a lack of discipline and accountability along with inappropriate behavior. That may be the case with others, but it resulted in one core (desired) outcome within our family dynamic.

Our daughters talked to us.

Not every day and not about every aspect of their lives. However, we often held open and honest conversations with our daughters about the most serious topics, issues, decisions, and challenges.

Second, the common response from a teenager is, "Yeah, sorry, but things are different now, Dad (or Mom). You don't understand what I deal with." Or similar. And this is when you must be open, honest, and vulnerable. We, as parents, know that, while technology and other things might change, the essence and emotions of being a teenager are the same. You must tell stories from your teenage years that your teenager can relate to—stories that deeply hurt and molded you. Stories you learned from.

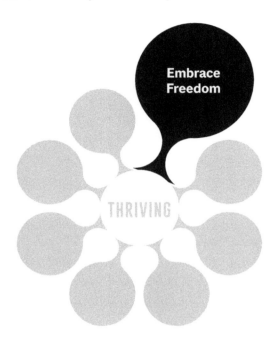

In summary, the combination of freedom (in exchange for conversation) and no pressure on grades, credentials, or what they would "be" created a relaxed atmosphere of mutual respect (usually, but not always). Our daughters were freed up from feeling like they had to fake their way through each day, which enabled them to be kids, have fun, and gradually discover who they were. Again, I accept that many parents are uncomfortable with such an approach and feel it is too "loosey-goosey," but that's how we decided to parent. I am convinced it (1) played a crucial role in why they're thriving as young adults and (2) enabled us to have deep and fulfilling relationships with each of them.

CHAPTER 24

Self-Direct

Self-direct learning and expectations

THRIVING

In our society, "school," "education," and "learning" get mixed and matched together. You go to school to get your education, which means you're learning. If you're not good at school, you're not learning; if you're not learning, you will not be educated; and if you're not educated, you won't amount to much of anything. Around and around it goes.

Upon exiting the education system, fifteen-plus years of pressure to "get good grades" results in an entrenched fixed mindset about learning. At school, learning is done to you. Someone else tells you what to learn and how to learn it. If you memorize what you're told, then you get recognition. This fixed mindset often prevents your teenager from becoming a dynamic and curious learner.

SELF-DIRECTED LEARNING

To begin, help your teenager understand there doesn't need to be any outcome other than learning. School causes students to associate learning with being rewarded or celebrated—the goal of learning is to get an A so that people will tell you you're smart or because it will enable you to get a job and make money later. But, when you strip away external or future rewards and self-direct your learning, the reward is attaining the knowledge you sought. Remember that picture of Brooke the day she learned how to ride a bike? Simply put, it feels good when you set out to learn something and then do so. You want your teenager to become addicted to that feeling because it will serve them well for the rest of their life. Rather than waiting to be told what to learn, they will, countless times, feel like that picture after learning something they choose to learn.

While you can and will learn things at school, the approach can result in bad habits that are hard to break later, such as waiting for someone else to tell you what to learn, that there is a start and end date to learning, that reading equals boring textbooks, or that you learn to be rewarded with a grade or future job.

We aim to ensure you take advantage of learning opportunities at school while resisting the bad habits that easily creep in.

We simply want you to be curious. You and I will regularly share what we're each curious about and why. Because I have a several-decade head start, I will suggest some things I think are good for you to learn and why—a few of those things will be required, but everything else will be up to you. And I hope you'll suggest things you think I should learn and why.

This is not a set-it-and-forget-it strategy. Once you establish this new approach to learning, the key is to develop a pattern of self-driven curiosity and constant discovery. It will not happen immediately; just stay at it.

For example, I strongly encouraged each of our daughters to read Carol Dweck's book, mentioned earlier. I often sent links to online content I thought would interest them and shared podcast episodes I knew they'd like. When I learned my oldest daughter was reading The Hunger Games trilogy, I also read and discussed the books with her. I established a rule in their teen years—for as long as I am alive, any book you buy is on me. We all share a Kindle account, and each of us reads and recommends books.

All that said, the one thing I did not do was force them to learn something. What tended to work better was to regularly strike up conversations with a question or two like these:

What is interesting to you? You get to pick anything, and the only unacceptable answer is "nothing." (Based on the answer:) Great, let's do some online searching and help you decide how you will start to learn about it.

What are a few things you learned this week on your own? What made you decide to learn ____ or ____ ?

Was there anything this week you expected to enjoy learning, only to discover it wasn't as interesting as you hoped? What did you not like about it? Why?

Of the things you learned this week, what did you find most surprising? Or amusing? Or disturbing?

What is the one thing you're most motivated to really deepen your learning about? Why?

This didn't require much effort or "thinking"—we just sat down, asked an open-ended question, and let it happen. Sometimes no one was in the mood, sometimes it was a five-minute exchange, and other times, we ended up in a two-hour conversation. Again, stay at it, and your teenager will start to engage. As they do, five things will shift them into high gear.

First, let them know where this is all going. While self-directed learning benefits teenagers, this is mostly about forming a mindset that will be applied throughout all aspects of life and be a significant enabler of their future happiness and fulfillment.

Self directed learning is the key to new skills and knowledge

By <u>Lois Melkonian</u>

January 31, 2022 - 16 MIN READ

Traditionally, academics contrast this to direct learning.

The direct learning meaning is straightforward. And the direct method is a common strategy for learning. It refers to educational instruction from a teacher to a learner, typically in a classroom setting.

But today, we're going to explore how much there is to gain from being a self-directed learner in <u>every area of your life</u>.

Figure 23. We often shared online content to help our daughters understand the value of self-directed learning.

(Source: Lois Melkonian, "Self Directed Learning Is the Key to New Skills and Knowledge," *BetterUp*, January 31, 2022. https://www.betterup.com/blog/self-directed-learning)

Second, avoid the temptation to set rules about what they can and cannot learn. Remember, it is called self-directed learning for a reason. Parents want to "protect" their children from knowing certain things, but if your teenager is determined to learn or know something, you *will not* stop them. So, don't try. Let it happen, and encourage them to talk to you about it.

Third, rather than try to influence what they learn, seek to understand what they want to learn and why. Remember, knowing something is different from applying what you know. Just because a teenager wants to learn how to make a bomb doesn't mean they want to hurt someone.

Fourth, while it's crucial that you not "take over" the learning, find subtle ways to help your teenager channel their energy. For example, start conversations like these:

What is an inherent strength you'd like to make even stronger? I don't care what it is—what makes you feel confident when you're doing it?

What is an inherent weakness you want to work on? What do you not like to do or feel uncomfortable doing, but you know you need to become at least average at it?

As we've discussed, don't worry about picking a career. But . . . if you could generate income tomorrow doing something, what would it be? What do you think you could learn to do well that would create value some people would be willing to pay for?

Going back to the first point above (where this is all going), while the learning itself is a great outcome, as your teenager moves into early adulthood, the goal is to ensure they have the self-confidence and drive to focus their learning. This empowers them to maximize their strengths, work on weaknesses, and achieve their version of success throughout life (I've repeatedly seen this play out with our daughters and will provide details later in this section).

Last, actively model the behavior. Showing your teenager that you practice what you preach might be the most impactful thing you can do. Share new things you learned and why you decided to learn them. Share how you're applying what you learned. Share what you can't wait to learn next. Ask your teenager if they recently learned something they think you should explore.

Do these things to unleash a vibrant, self-directed learner.

SELF-DIRECT EXPECTATIONS

Earlier, I shared a study about how the average college graduate's salary is almost fifty percent below their expectation, which is one of many false expectations the path creates. But your teenager will not be on the path, so you get to help them learn how to set their own expectations.

There will be times when you have little to no control over your reality (such as being told you have stage 3 cancer). However, you will always have control over the expectations you set for yourself and the people with whom you interact.

For example, as you enter adulthood, you will have expectations about things such as:

Financial: *How much money you **expect** to make and what lifestyle you **expect** to have.*

Location: *Where you **expect** to live and what you **expect** to have access to.*

Work: *What you **expect** to be paid to do or provide.*

Knowledge: *What you **expect** to learn and how you expect to learn it.*

Relationships: *The types of friends and partner(s) you **expect** to spend time with.*

Enjoyment: *What you **expect** to be able to experience or do that gives you joy.*

There might not be a more important skill than becoming adept at setting, adjusting, and achieving your expectations.

It takes time for people of any age to build the self-confidence to set, manage, and pivot their expectations, which is why you should start early. Here are six pieces of advice to guide your teenager:

1.   If you dream big, proceed with caution.
2.   You can't always get what you want.
3.   Don't pay attention to scare tactics.
4.   Set expectations based on something you did.
5.   Take on some risk here and there.
6.   Don't let other people set your expectations.

First, while it's perfectly fine to dream big, encourage your teenager to remember that the bigger their dreams, the bigger their expectations. And the bigger their expectations, the bigger their future reality must be to exceed those expectations. Remember . . . Happiness = Reality - Expectations.

For example, if you expect to be rich, famous, happily married, in perfect health, with a great figure and lots of friends . . . well, that's a hard reality to create. If that's how your teenager rolls—a big dreamer—so be it; encourage them to proceed cautiously.

Second, adults love to tell kids, "If you put your mind to it, you can do anything." I'm sorry, but that's meaningless hyperbole that rarely serves a purpose. As a fifty-three-year-old man who never played football, I cannot play in the NFL this season because I decided to put my mind to it. Help your teenager accept that determination and grit matter, but they can't always get what they want. That's life.

Third, when setting expectations for their future, ensure your teenager ignores the "data" about the supposed correlation between achievements now and as an adult. This is a scare tactic used to drive conformity. It's okay to be a kid; as discussed earlier, averages do not apply to individuals.

Fourth, the best way to set a new expectation is to base it on something you already did. For example, rather than expect to climb Mount Everest next week, climb a one-thousand-foot hill first, then set an expectation to climb a two-thousand-foot hill within a month. Rather than expect you will create a $10 million business within two years, create a $10,000 business first, then set an expectation to grow it to a $100,000 business in two years. You get the point. Encourage your teenager to take this approach, enabling them to build their confidence and be honest about what they can and cannot do (or even want or do not want to do).

Fifth, building off the earlier chapter on risk-taking, help your teenager set expectations with moderate risks that feel a bit scary. It's okay for them to feel nervous and unsure of themselves and the outcome—this is how they gain the necessary experience and mindset to pursue more significant rewards through more considerable risks. As a teenager, you'll be fine unless your mistakes cause an unrecoverable flat spin where Goose dies.

Last, constantly remind your teenager that people love to evaluate and "judge" the expectations of others—mainly when yours differ from theirs. While you should always listen to people you respect and who genuinely have your best interests in mind, you're the only person who hears the voice in your head. By far, the most critical aspect of expectation setting is that *you* set them. Yes, gather advice and listen to intelligent people, but do not allow someone else to set your expectations. That. Is. Critical.

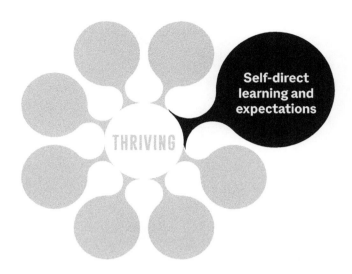

Close your eyes and envision your teenager actively and confidently self-directing their learning and expectation setting. Envision a collaborative process through which your teenager does this with you as a mentor and guide. *That* is what you're aiming for.

CHAPTER 25

Prioritize Emotional Intelligence

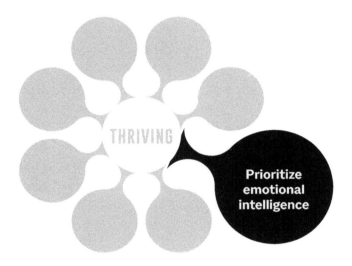

I'm a *huge* proponent of emotional intelligence (a.k.a. emotional quotient, or EQ) and think it's foundational to thriving at any age. Still, I'm far from a trailblazer in that position. There are gobs of research and opinion pieces that validate the importance of EQ in virtually all aspects of life. I encourage you to learn EQ from top to bottom because you *must* infuse every aspect of it into your teenager.

ICONS & INNOVATORS

Richard Branson Says EQ Is More Important Than IQ for Success Don't let less-than-stellar academic performance hold you back from your dreams, Branson urges. A boatload of science backs him up.

BY JESSICA STILLMAN, CONTRIBUTOR, INC.COM @ENTRYLEVELREBEL

Figure 24. Business leaders value emotional intelligence over book smarts, and science backs them up.

(Source: Jessica Stillman, "Richard Branson Says EQ Is More Important than IQ for Success," *Inc.*, July 18, 2023. https://www.inc.com/jessica-stillman/richard-branson-says-eq-is-more-important-than-iq-for-success-science-suggests-hes-right.html)

Much of what you will find regarding EQ centers on career development, executive leadership, and so forth. These are all important, of course, but typically not relevant for a teenager. Thus, the key is to find ways to put EQ in the context of what your teenager experiences daily and to help them understand its importance. We simplified EQ for our teenage daughters and encouraged them to focus on themselves first. The primary goal was to help them develop their EQ such that they did not allow their emotions or the emotions of others to impact their self-worth and decision-making. We used four questions to foster their development.

QUESTION 1

Over the last few weeks or months, tell me about a couple of times when you became highly emotional—when you were triggered. Okay, great. As you think about these examples and others, what are the common characteristics? Are there any patterns?

EQ starts with self-awareness. All of us—even the most accomplished adults with high EQ—get triggered. And different things trigger different people in different ways. What sets you off might be hardly noticeable to me and vice versa.

To begin with, help your teenager learn their triggers. If they struggle to share their personal triggers, model the behavior and share yours. Tell them about moments you were overly emotional and why. It might take some time, but if you model the behavior, your teenager will eventually settle in. Building EQ requires self-awareness about when they're being triggered and why. Start there.

QUESTION 2

We talked about recent moments when you were triggered. Now, think back to a situation or event at least one year ago that caused extreme emotions. Tell me what it was and how you felt. Don't hold anything back.

Okay, thank you for sharing that. If your emotions were a ten out of ten at that time, how high are they today regarding that specific event or situation? What impact did it have on your life today?

Over time, if your teenager shares genuine examples, they will learn that while emotions can be powerful and sometimes feel overwhelming, they're almost always temporary. I also encourage you to proactively look for situations in which your teenager is highly emotional about something that feels like the end of the world. Enter a quick note in your phone describing the situation, set a reminder for one year later, and then hold the same conversation above.

When a highly emotional event happens, a person with high EQ will immediately think about how they have experienced similar emotions that dissipate over time. High EQ shows up when your teenager can tell you about a situation where they started to feel triggered but immediately thought, "This too shall pass."

QUESTION 3

 So far, we have focused on your emotions and how you felt in a moment, but now I was hoping you could think about any decisions you made in those moments. What are a couple of things you said or did while emotionally triggered? As you sit here today (not highly charged or triggered), how effective was that decision-making? If you could undo anything, what would it be?

This is when you help your teenager understand a key "why" behind EQ—decision-making.

I can recall bad decisions I made that created anything from chaos to unhappiness to distress to pain. And those bad decisions were often made when I was emotionally triggered. When we're emotionally charged, snap decisions, actions, words, and deeds often cause regret. The next step in your teenager's EQ development is to postpone decision-making until their emotions are calm. The point isn't to tell them to remove all emotion from their decisions but to be aware of their emotions and assess how they are helping or harming what they're trying to accomplish or decide.

As previously shared, the upside to making mistakes as a teenager is that almost none of them will "ruin" you. The sooner (and more often) your teenager learns to carefully assess if a decision should be made when they're emotionally triggered, the (far) more likely they are to become good decision-makers as young adults. Good choices are like compounding interest—over time, they stack together and lead to lots of goodness. And the opposite is true as well.

QUESTION 4

It's always important to remember that human beings are like icebergs—you only see a small percentage of their entirety. I want you to think back on situations in which you felt another person was acting irrationally or poorly and judged them as "being" the way they were acting. With any of those situations, have you since been able to get to know that person and understand why they might have acted that way?

This is when you help your teenager transition from a self-focused perspective to using EQ in their interactions with others. Some people are irrational and unreasonable, and you will not change them. Your teenager should avoid those people at all costs. But most people's behavior is driven by complex, unseen factors like memories, instincts, fears, and selfish motives. Things they know, feel, and rue while those around them have no idea.

It's essential to help your teenager understand that when someone is angry, it might mean they are dissatisfied with something your teen said/did, or it could be because they got yelled at by a parent that morning, or it could be a deep-seated issue they're not even aware is impacting their emotions. As your teenager improves at understanding this, they will build more empathy toward others and themselves. They'll be more forgiving and not harbor or carry as much negativity. And that is tremendously important.

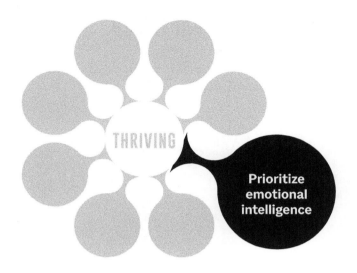

THRIVING

Prioritize emotional intelligence

Again, I'm all in on EQ and believe a person's success and happiness are primarily driven by being aware of and controlling their emotions. The message to your teenager is *not* to be a robot who feels nothing. That is not the point. The point is to help them be self-aware about when they're feeling emotionally charged, why, and what to do (and not do) in those moments. Our daughters strongly believe their emotional intelligence, developed since their early teen years, sets them apart as young adults. High EQ enables them to reduce stress, release negative thoughts, make decisions calmly, compound good decisions, and consistently find happiness.

CHAPTER 26

Do What Makes You Feel Accomplished

Most parents seek an ambitious and driven teenager. They want their teen to demonstrate a strong work ethic, find things they're passionate about, get good grades, and strive for achievements. Then, they venture off to college, find their identity, acquire an all-important credential, and transition into adulthood. It's a master plan that works for some, but I never believed in it. Too expensive, formulaic, and linear.

That brings us back to Brooke. At nineteen, she
- graduated high school with a 2-point-something GPA,
- achieved zero merits, awards, or external recognition,
- dropped out of college after one semester,
- languished at home with low self-confidence and no direction,
- earned the nickname "Pig-Pen" for her slovenly nature,
- held a grand total of one part-time job for four months,
- was severely overweight with terrible eating habits,
- rarely exercised or spent time outside, and
- didn't have the first inclination about a career.

After an ultimatum from her parents, over the next four years, she
- left home and moved into her own apartment,
- kept her living space organized and immaculately clean,
- rescued and bonded with her first dog,
- selected a desired lifestyle and built a budget to attain it,
- started a successful small business,
- started working full-time in a job she loves,
- achieved financial independence,
- transitioned from directionless to self-directed,
- became passionate about health and fitness,
- taught herself how to cook healthy meals she enjoys,
- established a daily exercise routine and lost eighty pounds,
- built a life together with the person she will marry, and
- became a grounded, self-confident, and thriving young adult.

It is a remarkable transformation over a four-year period, but it started and was consistently driven by the title of this chapter, which she mentioned in a text message I shared earlier.

> I had to go from feeling no motivation, no direction, just simply "existing" to finding what makes me want to get out of bed every day feeling motivated and then go to sleep feeling accomplished.

Path-following parents relentlessly insist their teens do and determine things, but most of it is "fake hustle" that means nothing in the long run. Being an adult is entirely different from being a kid. Once your child exits the teen years and enters independence, they will find happiness if they're fully empowered and able to take ownership of what causes them to consistently go to bed feeling accomplished and wake up feeling excited about the day ahead.

If you're not convinced, maybe Brooke's journey will move the pendulum. One quick point upfront—Brooke is not and may never be in a traditional corporate career, and if you are determined that your teenager must be in such a career, I will say two things. First, it's not about what you want—focus on helping your teenager decide what *they* want. Second, Lauren is in a corporate career, and I'll lay out her steps at the end of this section.

ULTIMATUM AND FIRST STEPS

Six months after dropping out of college, Brooke continued to regress. My wife and I decided the safety and security of living at home enabled her regression. I took her to dinner and delivered an ultimatum.

The whole point of not going to/dropping out of college is to enable you to focus on yourself—to actively start to work on who you are, to start doing things to earn income, to explore your strengths and weaknesses, etc. You admit you lack motivation and feel unhappy and lost, but you won't proactively do anything representing forward progress.

We are confident you have the right mindset and lots of value to offer the world, but you need a push. With that in mind, you have thirty days to devise a plan to move out of the house, and within ninety days you must move out. If you don't present your own plan within thirty days, we will present our plan, which you must follow.

Yep, we kicked her out of the house, but it is important to note three things about our decision. First, starting in middle school, we told our daughters that we could either pay for college or, if they chose not to go, they would gain access to the money (with our guidance) we would have spent to send them (if this isn't financially possible for you, I address an alternate approach in the next chapter). With that in mind, we told Brooke she would receive $500 monthly from the "college" fund and needed to earn enough money to pay for the rest of her living needs.

Second, we weren't kicking her out with no reprieve. Although we gave her no choice about trying it, we clarified that if things didn't work out after a few months, she could move back home, regroup, and try again (she never had to). This eased her stress early on.

Last, her track record and lack of path-based achievements to that point in her life would cause few people to expect her to thrive immediately. And we wouldn't have been surprised if she had to move back home at least once. However, we forced her hand because we were highly confident she possessed a growth mindset, high emotional intelligence, and many valuable traits she hadn't been able to apply.

That dinner changed everything. Less than a week later, Brooke presented her plan, and a few weeks later, she moved into a one-bedroom apartment. From there, the transition immediately started. Every time we interacted with her during that college semester or the six months after she dropped out, she seemed to lose ground. But after moving out, each interaction made it clear she had taken a step forward.

Her first conscientious decision was to keep her apartment immaculately clean, which was quite a change from her previous mindset at home (thus, the Pig-Pen nickname). When she looked around before going to bed and immediately after waking up, a clean apartment gave her a sense of accomplishment. Within a few weeks, she discovered that being responsible for her schedule and living space wasn't so scary. Her cost of living was super low, and she immediately enjoyed the freedom, telling us, "I like this, I don't want to move back home, I want to be in control of what I do." This was incredibly important for her self-confidence.

A pattern was emerging. One thing leads to another.

TAKING CONTROL AND FINDING PURPOSE

As Brooke shifted out of fear and trepidation about living independently, she started to evaluate her day-to-day activity and adjust. First, being "in control of what I do" meant she needed a budget to manage spending. We helped a bit, but she found lots of free information online and quickly learned the basics of financial awareness. Operating within a budget enabled her to learn the cost of things (the focus of the next chapter), especially the high cost of ordering food. That led to learning how to cook (just the basics to save money) by watching YouTube videos and scrolling Pinterest for recipes (a simple example of how the internet enables self-directed learning). Financial awareness and cooking for herself built confidence and added more reasons to feel accomplished.

Her next decision was a game-changer in multiple ways. Brooke always loved dogs. Every time we took her for a walk as a toddler, we knew that, with each dog we passed, we'd hear, "Can I pet your dog?" Though she grew up with a dog in the house, she decided to rescue a dog that would 100 percent be her responsibility. Her immediate bond with Lola (a Swiss mountain dog) gave her life a new and vital purpose. She had to wake up at 7:00 a.m. (vs. 10:00 or 11:00 a.m.), and while previously stagnant and inside much of the time, she had to go outside to walk Lola several times a day.

Figure 25.
Brooke out on a walk with her favorite creature, Lola.

Most importantly, she gained confidence and purpose by caring for this new creature she loved dearly.

GETTING ORGANIZED AND EXPANDING ACTIVITIES

Brooke was putting things together during what would have been the first half of her sophomore year in college. The "extra" hours each day waking up early with Lola caused her to think about how to use those hours to increase her income. In parallel, being outside and active caused her to realize how much better she felt and motivated her to invest more in her health and exercise. With an increasing number of activities happening or planned, she learned (again for free) how to create a time-management system (a notorious weakness as a teenager). Feeling organized reduced her stress and led to many "Wow, I got a lot done today" moments of fulfillment.

Based on online research, she decided to experiment with making and selling candles. A $200 kit and several hours of trial and error produced her first batch of five scents, which she gave to friends, family and coworkers. The positive feedback motivated her to start a candle-making business (Swissy Wicks her Mom came up with the name) with $1,000 of initial cash flow from the college fund (a tiny percentage).

Figure 26. One of Brooke's hand-made candles, which she sold online and in person.

Interestingly, she now needed to learn things that previously bored her to tears in school, such as accounting, inventory management, packaging design, and pricing. It's a different level of investment when you choose and immediately apply what you learn to something important to you. Each online course was less than $50 with no tests or grades—because what is the point of grades when you're already highly motivated to learn?

Last, motivated to increase her income through a part-time job at a boutique retailer, she approached the store owner and stated a desire to deliver more value through increased sales. She asked for advice and coaching, applied what she was taught, paid more attention to details, and became the top seller on the floor.

In what would have been the first half of her junior year in college, Brooke was crushing it. Instead of attending classes, studying for tests, and experiencing the college scene, she was figuring herself out, building her candle business, enjoying dog ownership, and increasing her income. She told us about twelve months after moving out, "You can stop giving me the $500 a month—I got it now." She reached financial independence at twenty and has remained so ever since.

The pattern was now in full flight. One thing leads to another.

THRIVING

In July 2021, Brooke sought full-time work as a nanny and shut down her candle business. While she learned a lot, enjoyed the experience, and made some decent money, she didn't want to run a business full-time. As we had told her since middle school, that was fine—never get stuck doing something you don't want to do. In parallel, her physical fitness became a top priority. She invested in expanding her cooking prowess for healthy meals (again, all for free online) and committed to one hour of exercise daily.

She landed a full-time position as a nanny with a great family she remains with today, moved into (and furnished) a house with more space and a backyard for Lola, bought her first car, and got engaged to a young man we are happy to welcome into our family. The "college" fund enabled her to do all of this without taking on a single dollar of debt, and she *still* has a good bit of money left over (yes, college is insanely expensive).

When her friends from high school were graduating college, entering the real world, and starting to face the realities of adulting, Brooke was a thriving young adult rocking a growth mindset—grounded, mature, calm, driven, happy, independent, and confident. In just about every way possible, she had found herself. In addition to many new friendships formed after high school, she's enjoyed visiting or hosting her childhood friends, who all went to college (of course). College can be a great social experience, but not going to college doesn't prevent you from making new friends or maintaining long-term friendships.

These days, Brooke makes decorative cakes as a side hustle and has created social media channels to make and share videos

Figure 27. Brooke and her fiancé, Sean.

Figure 28. Brooke making and sharing one of her healthy meals via social media.

for healthy recipes and meal prep/planning tips (you can find her at @cook_with_brooke_ on TikTok and Instagram; don't forget that last _). For now, it's a passion project she enjoys doing, with the added benefit of learning how to edit video content (an excellent skill to learn).

When I recently asked Brooke if she could have done any of these things four years ago, she said:

> There is no way I would have done any of this in the months after dropping out of college because I had little to no confidence. For example, I don't think anything could've convinced me to record myself and then post it to the world. But, today, I love doing that.

And when I asked about her plan with her social media channels:

> Aside from a tripod and maybe a couple of other pieces of equipment, I won't be investing money in this. Just time. I'm so passionate about my personal weight loss journey and health in general that I could see this going somewhere. But if it doesn't, no biggie. I have fun filming and even editing so I'm not really losing anything even if this doesn't go anywhere.

The essence of a growth mindset.

There was never a grandiose plan for either of our daughters to invest eight years and tons of money pursuing academic excellence and accumulating credentials. No need to be "suitable for something."

While it took a push to flip the switch, Brooke used her strong foundation (growth mindset, emotional intelligence, self-directed learning/expectation-setting) and gradually learned how to do

THRIVING

Do what makes you feel accomplished

things that make her feel happy and accomplished. It didn't happen overnight; instead, it was a slow burn as she transitioned from kid to adult. Looking ahead, she might try to build a brand based on her personal journey, keep making videos for fun, expand her cake making, or transition from a nanny to a different kind of full-time work. Who knows?

It's okay to stop doing what everyone else tells you and, instead, own your story and build confidence by doing what you want. When you take that approach, a beautiful pattern takes shape.

One thing leads to another.

FAQS I HEAR OR CAN PREDICT

Will Brooke want the stability of an established career at some point? What does that even mean? People in "established" careers get fired or laid off. The only financial stability Brooke seeks is earning more than she spends for her desired lifestyle. Whenever she becomes motivated to increase her income, she finds ways to make it happen. That's her mindset.

Is she making lots of money? Compared to some people, yes, compared to others, no. She makes more money each month than she spends, lives a financially comfortable life with zero debt, and sees no reason to pursue more money just for the sake of it.

Does she do any networking? Nah, not in the traditional sense. As she dabbles with building a brand based on her health journey, she teaches herself how to "network" via social media. And she presents her cakes on Facebook, Instagram, and TikTok, but that's about it.

Does she feel she missed out on the "once-in-a-lifetime" college experience? Oh my gosh, not in the least bit. Within a few weeks, she knew college was a harmful environment for her at that time, causing her to take steps backward. She has thoroughly enjoyed self-development in a "quiet" way. It fits her.

What will she be doing in five years? She has no idea and wastes no time worrying about it. She leans into the uncertainty of life, doesn't worry about things outside of her control, and focuses on feeling accomplished each day.

CHAPTER 27

Learn the Cost of Things

Too many parents have it backward.

They fixate on how much money their teenager will make in Career A versus Career B versus Career C. "If you go into this career, you'll make about this amount of money, but if you go into this other one you'll probably make less." That's the wrong thing to focus on because your teen cannot "test" what life will be like when investing forty-plus hours a week to earn x amount of money versus y. They cannot "feel" what type of lifestyle x amount of money will enable versus y.

We encouraged our daughters to take the opposite approach—understand what things cost based on a desired lifestyle and *then* evaluate options to generate enough income to fund that lifestyle. In parallel, their college decision needed to be made based on a clear understanding of how much it costs and how that money could be applied if they chose not to go.

We live in a money-obsessed society. If you travel internationally or, at minimum, read about the rest of the world, you will learn that not all societies operate this way. But ours does. It's just the reality.

Following the path doubles down on this mindset. It leads to a fixation on pursuing money via a "good job" in a high-paying career. It starts with your parents, gets amped through the media, and is reinforced by the adults in your life. If left unchecked, you will be obsessed with chasing money and job titles.

But you're not following the path and learned not to be influenced or manipulated by the media. You get to take a better approach.

To be clear—there is nothing wrong with pursuing money to acquire material things and your desired lifestyle. The problem is when (1) the pursuit of money leads to unhappiness (i.e., when you hear adults say their self-identity is tied to their job) and (2) unhappy people pursue money, hoping it will make them happy.

We're going to flip the script. Learn how to be happy first. Then, pursue money—and a specific career—if and only if it will maintain and/or increase your happiness.

I know this sounds fluffy—rainbows and unicorns, we want everyone to be happy—but remember what I shared at the start of this book. Far too many young adults are unhappy. They do not feel accomplished and self-confident when their heads hit the pillow at night. Instead, they often feel stressed, anxious, and, at times, overwhelmed. I always felt the best way for a teenager to prepare for the real world is to start living in the real world, but with the kind of bumper rails kids use at bowling alleys. They are not ready to bowl a strike with each ball, but they will not wind up in the gutter.

START WITH $10,000

Most teenagers go to college with the mindset of "I'll be on my own for the first time," but we helped our daughters understand that's a myth. We did not want them to believe existing in a bubble for four years would, in any way, prepare them for what full-time adulting looks like.

- The effort, focus, and time required to generate income in a full-time job.
- What you have left in the tank after your responsibilities at work (i.e., the balance between how much your job rewards and motivates you versus drains and sucks the life out of you).
- What you have left in the tank after your responsibilities outside your full-time job.
- What you have left in the tank as "me time" after caring for work and responsibilities.
- How effectively you invest "me time" in activities that truly fulfill you.
- Your personal happiness and fulfillment after the dust settles.

As parents, we know that is our daily challenge, and it's a tricky puzzle to solve even when we're only focused on ourselves. College does very little to prepare your teenager for it. Instead, building on the above-mentioned conversation, introduce three ways your teenager can acquire enough money ($10,000) to invest a few months (at minimum) in learning the cost of things before making the monumental decision to invest in college.

First, a fourteen-year-old can easily earn $100/week (much more if highly motivated), and even if they spend half of what they make, $10,000 will be saved by the age of eighteen. Second, if they start late or do not earn $10,000 by high school graduation, they can live at home and work full-time since they no longer spend time on school or school-related activities. They can easily make $15 to $20 an hour as a server at a restaurant and, even if starting with no savings, can get to $10,000 within six to eight months. Third, if financially able, give your high school graduate access to $10,000 (a tiny percentage of the cost of a four-year degree) so they can start immediately.

Category	Monthly	Notes
Rent	$1,025	Small, 1-bedroom apartment near local university
Auto-Gas	$100	She drove a 10-year-old car we bought her when she turned 16
General 'Fun' and Entertainment	$150	She tried to really limit this, which led to learning to cook
Utilities	$75	Rent included water/sewer, gas, internet, satalite tv & trash – she paid for electricity
Clothes / Shopping	$125	She did need clothes for work, but tried to bargain shop as much as possible
Groceries	$350	This increased when she got Lola
Misc	$100	Everything else
Total Monthly Cost of Living	$1,925	
Minus $500 / Month Stipend	-$500	From the "if you'd gone to college" fund
Net Monthly Cost of Living to Cover	$1,425	
Monthly Income She Needed to Generate	$1,781	Assume 20% tax rate on income

*We paid her monthly mobile phone bill and car insurance, and she was covered under my company's health insurance

Figure 29. Brooke's first budget after moving out on her own.

In parallel to your teenager earning $10,000, explain the cost of things and build confidence by creating a simple budget. Brooke made this one a few months after moving out of our house into a one-bedroom apartment.

Adjust the budget based on where you live and give your teenager confidence that living independently is not as scary and daunting as they might think. Brooke was fortunate enough to have an "if you'd gone to college" fund, and your teenager might as well, but if not, this is when their $10,000 comes into play. Their cost of living will be so low that they can use that money to relieve pressure as they initially venture out into the real world (for example, $10,000 will last twenty months with a $500-per-month stipend).

Once your teenager ventures out and gets started, they'll quickly build confidence and work their way into things. For example, Brooke's $500-per-month stipend left her only needing to earn ~$1,800/month before taxes, which meant she had options such as:

- Work forty hours per week at $11.25/hour.
- Be a restaurant server, work five weekly shifts, and average $75 to $80/shift in tips.
- Work twenty-five hours per week in a boutique retailer at $10/ hour, averaging another $200/week in commission (based on the amount of merchandise sold) and selling candles.

She chose the third option and consistently generated the necessary income from day one to support herself. She was not, by any means, living la vida loca, but (this is the key) once she started to understand the cost of things, trade-offs materialized. For example, after two years in an apartment, she wanted a house with more space and a fenced-in yard, which meant higher rent and utilities. The status quo wouldn't cut it—she needed to increase income and tighten spending.

Waking up earlier to walk Lola created new "earning" hours. Cooking for herself saved money versus eating out, but she often went out with friends. She cut back, which helped, but it wasn't enough. This was when she started making candles, applied extra effort at her part-time job, and eventually shifted to full-time work. By learning the cost of things, she made decisions, set expectations, and worked toward her desired income level. *That* is what becoming an adult looks like. Worst-case scenario—they'll learn the cost of living in the real world and navigate trade-offs to achieve a desired lifestyle. Based on this newfound knowledge, your teenager can make a college decision based on its "real" cost.

THE REAL COST OF COLLEGE

Our direction to Brooke and Lauren was that college, even if it were free, is not a no-brainer decision. Of course, college is far from free. Earlier, I introduced the four types of cost—hard, soft, time, and opportunity—and discussed how college is a high-risk bet because the opportunity cost is incalculable. Well, let's try to calculate it by starting with some simple math.

	Tuition & Fees	Room & Board	Books & Supplies	Travel & Other Expenses	Total
Public College (two-year, in-district)	$3,860	$9,610	$1,460	$4,300	$19,230
Public College (four-year, in-state)	$10,940	$12,310	$1,240	$3,400	$27,940
Public College (four-year, out-of-state)	$28,240	$12,310	$1,240	$3,450	$45,240
Private College (not-for-profit)	$39,400	$14,030	$1,240	$2,900	$57,570

Figure 30. Average cost of college in the 2023–2024 school year.

(Source: "Estimating the True Cost of College in 2023," *College Ave*, October 17, 2022. https://www.collegeave.com/articles/estimating-the-true-cost-of-college/)

As Figure 30 shows, the all-in cost of a four-year college degree ranges from $28,000 per year ($112,000 total) for an in-state public school to $57,500 per year ($230,000 total) for a private college. Think about that. We just talked about how far a teenager can go on their own, starting out with just $10,000; imagine what they can do with access to $112,000 or even $230,000. I cannot understand why parents and teenagers commit to college without discussing the total cost and exploring alternatives.

First, pick an all-in cost based on factors such as where you live, financial aid, scholarships, travel to and from home, sorority/fraternity fees, and other aspects specific to your situation. I will use $140,000 ($35,000/year) for this exercise, but the approach is the same no matter what amount you choose.

Start with putting this cost into a simple context your teenager will understand—the hourly rate. Since a college student spends about eight months per year "active" at college, that nets out to 34 weeks per year and 136 weeks over four years. If we assume a standard 40-hour work week, those 136 weeks equal 5,440 hours (136 weeks * 40 hours per week), and when we divide those 5,440 hours into the total cost of $140,000, the hourly rate is $25 per hour. Help your teenager internalize this reality. Imagine giving someone $25 of money you worked hard to earn, then again an hour from now, and then again two hours from now, and then again—for 5,440 hours in a row.

But it gets worse.

While at college, you spend time on activities that do not generate income. Again, if we assume the average work week is 40 hours, a college student can easily earn $15 to $20 per hour, or like Lauren, you could land your first full-time position at the age of twenty and earn $30 per hour or more. The "real" cost of college is what you spend plus what you could make. So, now, imagine handing over $45 to someone else, then again after one hour, then again . . . for 5,440 hours. In this scenario, the "real" cost of college is $250,000 (5,440 hours * $45/hour)—a quarter of a million dollars! If you choose to go to an out-of-state school, it approaches $350,000 to $400,000. If you go to a private school, it approaches $500,000.

But it gets worse.

In addition to the cost of college from a purely monetary perspective, there are the "soft" costs of stress, anxiety, and worry over several years, plus the focused self-development and learning (what I just walked through with Brooke) that you cannot do because of everything college requires. Your numbers will vary, and the range from the above might be significant. Still, please take the time to evaluate the all-in "real" cost of college with your teenager.

No matter how we run the numbers, the total cost of college (hard, soft, and opportunity) is so high that the investment will only make sense in a few scenarios. There may be a scenario that applies specifically to you, but a massive investment like this should only be made after thoroughly researching and evaluating all options.

As always, when considering the value propositions of college, we will remember that you no longer need to pay for knowledge you can acquire for free or even get paid to learn. You no longer need to learn from people who supposedly know how to do things because you can easily find and learn from people doing those things. You no longer need to pay to build a network, and there are many ways to have fun and build lifelong relationships through experiences of your own choosing.

We may discover a scenario in which the total cost of college is a solid bet to make, but odds are we find a much less expensive and better option for you to try first.

To close this chapter, I encourage you to revisit the sample budget created earlier. With your specific financial situation in mind, consider either or both of the following scenarios.

SCENARIO 1: STUDENT LOANS

For many families, sending a child to college requires student loans, and you must explain what this means using context a teenager can understand. Do an online search for a debt repayment calculator, choose an amount to borrow, and pull back up the sample budget from earlier in this chapter. Again, the amount to be borrowed is specific to your situation, but I will use $75,000 for this exercise, with an interest rate of six percent.

Based on that amount and interest rate, a monthly payment of $537.32 will require twenty years to pay off the loan, and the total amount paid will be $129,000 ($75,000 of principal plus $54,000 in interest fees). A monthly payment of $632.89 will require fifteen years, and the total amount paid will be $114,000 ($39,000 in interest fees). Add the interest fees to the hourly cost of college. For example, if you end up paying $54,000 in interest, the hourly cost of those 5,440 hours goes up by another $10 per hour.

Now, refer to the budget and help your teenager understand what $600 a month will "feel" like. Show them what kind of car they could drive with a $600 monthly payment. Show them what trips they could take every three months for $1,800. Show them the difference in the apartment type they can rent with $1,500 per month versus $2,100 per month. Show them how quickly they will save enough for a down payment on a house if they invest $600 monthly.

Please do not allow your teenager to take out student loan debt without helping them understand relevant context and examples based on their situation and likely outcomes.

SCENARIO 2: NO LOANS

In the second scenario, your teenager is fortunate enough (like Brooke and Lauren) to have money set aside to go to college without student loans. For example, instead of needing to take out $75,000 in student loans, they can choose to go to college and deplete that money or choose not to go to college and gain access to that money with your oversight and guidance. Very few parents make this option available to their teenagers, but I highly encourage it.

Instead of an online debt repayment calculator, search for an online savings withdrawal calculator and enter a starting amount (such as $75,000), the annual rate of return you expect to earn, and a monthly withdrawal amount.

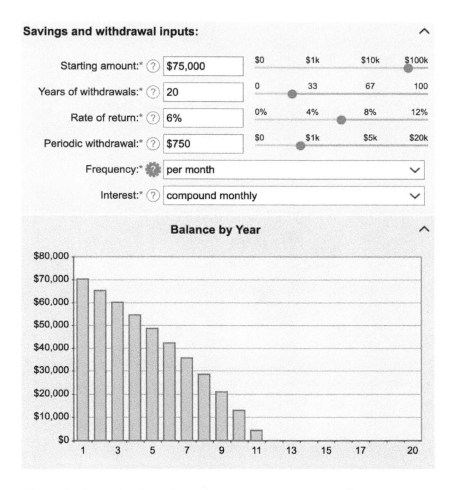

Figure 31. Example of a savings withdrawal calculator I use (from http://www.annuityexpertadvice.com.)

For example, invest $75,000 and earn an average of 6 percent interest annually (historical average investing in the stock market is ~8 percent). If so, your teenager will get access to $750 per month for almost eleven years. Or, instead, they could get access to $1,000 per month for nearly seven years. Again, going back to the sample budget, help them understand what this means and how much pressure is removed when they get access to this type of money *every* month as they start out in the real world.

THRIVING

Learn the cost of things

Even if you believe it uniquely delivers certain value propositions, it is irresponsible to blindly send your teenager to college without helping them understand the total cost. What is the rush? Why is it so critically important that teenagers go straight off to college after graduating high school? Why must a teenager be ready to start a career at twenty-two versus twenty-three or twenty-four?

Please help your teenager learn the cost of things and experiment a bit. These conversations and experiences are eye-opening because they allow your teenager to (finally) understand both the cost of living in the real world and the opportunity cost of choosing college. Trust me, it represents an engaging and impactful dialogue between parent and teen.

CHAPTER 28

Find Your Game

Many people hear Brooke's journey and think, "Sure, anyone can be a nanny or go into a trade and make a decent living. But for those wanting to maximize their high-end potential and earning, a college degree is the singular credential that removes all ceilings and raises all floors."

Nope.

I will dedicate these last chapters to walking through Lauren's journey. Now twenty-six, she lives in San Diego, California, and has a corporate job with a Fortune 200 company, high salary, fantastic benefits, and unlimited career potential. In calendar year 2023, she took forty flights (most for free) to destinations worldwide while simultaneously loving her job, coworkers, and company culture. She is experiencing the *exact* lifestyle she was told would be inaccessible without a college degree.

And here's the kicker—she did this without ever stressing about grades in high school, biting her nails hoping to be picked by a college, or feeling intense pressure to decide what she wanted to "be" for the rest of her life. At the risk of oversimplifying, there were four phases to her journey:

- **Phase 1:** She worked on many principles from this book during high school, preparing to pursue a corporate career of some type (not yet worried about which one).
- **Phase 2:** Post-high school, she (with help—I'll explain) went through a trial-and-error process to find her game.
- **Phase 3:** She built an initial skill set and portfolio and landed her first full-time job at twenty in the field she chose as her career starting point.
- **Phase 4:** She rapidly expanded her network and portfolio, focused on value creation, worked in three different industries, and landed her "dream job" at twenty-three.

We covered the first phase, so let's start with the second: how she found her game. Her first step after high school was participation in a program called UnCollege (no longer active). Today, a career development program called Praxis (do an online search for "discover praxis" to find them) is a great alternative. If you can afford or finance the cost, I highly recommend it.

SEEKING THREE CHARACTERISTICS

Programs like Praxis help their students learn desirable soft skills while going through a process to identify strengths and interests. For Lauren, this was the first step to finding her game—evaluating her abilities and strengths while seeking a combination of three characteristics.

1. I'm naturally good at this.
2. I enjoy doing and learning this.
3. There are in-demand jobs or careers that value this.

The goal is to find all three. Being good at something doesn't matter if you don't enjoy doing it, and similarly, thoroughly enjoying something doesn't mean there is high demand for that skill. You want to start with something that fits all three characteristics, and you'll likely need to experiment (which you cannot do in college).

For example, Lauren thought she would be good at coding and attended a boot camp in high school. After learning the basics and starting to write code, it was clear she could be good at it; however, she also felt bored and disinterested. She wasn't innately driven to learn and get better at coding, so she stopped. After all, there is no reason to "fake" interest or study for hours to learn something that doesn't interest you, right? Right?

At UnCollege, she worked with a mentor to identify and categorize what she was naturally good at and found interesting—and then experimented. She had a natural creative streak and was always curious about designs. Enjoyed problem-solving and loved doing puzzles. Good with numbers. Paid extra attention to signs, menu designs, and other elements that others didn't notice. Things like that caused an initial focus on web and graphic design. Her mentor gave her an assignment: "Over the next three days, I want you to write down at least ten things you notice." It turned out that most of her list was how things were packaged, which led them to explore packaging design as a potential start to her career. She took on a project to develop a fake product and design the packaging, and she enjoyed the process. Maybe she had found her game!

LETDOWN FOLLOWED BY A REVELATION

But . . . then came characteristic three: Was this a high-demand role? Lauren contacted a designer and offered to take her to coffee to learn more about the job. That conversation helped her understand that packaging design was a highly niche role and that it was hard to get a first job, which was disappointing but good to know. However, this person asked what elements of packaging design appealed to her and recommended a related field called UX/ UI (User Research/User Interface), explaining that it required many of the same skills and problem-solving elements Lauren enjoyed.

Figure 32. Six months after graduating from high school, Lauren felt she might have found her game with UX/UI Design.

(Source: Jess Feldman, "The UX Design Career Path," *Course Report*, September 1, 2021. https://www. coursereport.com/blog/the-ux-design-career-path-with-designlab)

Lauren started watching online videos and attended an in-person seminar about UX/UI. While initially skeptical (she found the seminar boring), the more she investigated, the more it felt she might be onto something. The role was quickly evolving, in demand, and with high compensation.

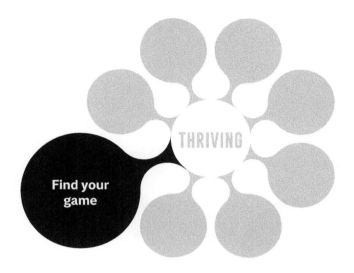

Finding your game is not about deciding what you want to "be." That approach is nonsensical when a teenager has zero real-world experience and is still early in self-discovery. For a teenager ready to generate income, it's about deciding what you want to try *first*. As life evolves, it's about determining what you want to try *next*.

A program like Praxis is a fantastic option if you can afford or finance the cost. It was perfect for someone like Lauren (not Brooke), who wanted to identify and start a corporate career after high school. Best of all, because it only requires twenty hours per week, there is plenty of time to earn money and focus on self-development.

Within the equivalent time frame of one semester of college, Lauren knew what she wanted to try first.

CHAPTER 29

Try Before You Buy

Lauren was ready to invest in learning the necessary skills to be a UX/UI Designer but spent no time evaluating it as what she wanted to "be." Because she didn't need to. Again, what's the point? As her high school peers were starting the second semester of their first year in college, our conversation went as follows:

I'm excited that four months of self-evaluation and discovery led to a potential option for getting a job and starting a career. UX/UI sounds like a great fit and worth a surgical investment of time and money, which you can do because you're not wasting time and money on general education courses on a college campus.

Over the next few weeks and months, find focused courses and boot camps, talk with UX/UI Designers, and, if possible, shadow one of them to see what the job looks like daily. In other words, try before you buy. If you discover that the more you learn, the more you want to keep learning, great. If not, no problem. Pivot your focus and attention to something else and keep exploring.

There is no rush—it's all about trial and error because you should never settle for work you do not find interesting, challenging, and fun.

For many, this feels risky, scary, and unrealistic. The safer, lower-risk approach is to pick a career before you fully understand or have tried it, invest gobs of money sitting in classrooms for 1,000s of hours trying to retain information you cannot yet apply, and then venture out and hope you made the right decision. Yep, that's way better.

Whatever.

After this conversation, Lauren stayed up most of that night researching boot camps and compiled options in a spreadsheet she was ready to discuss the following morning. At this moment, I knew she fully grasped self-directed learning and expectation setting. Although we were helping to guide her, she was driving this.

We discussed each option, and she settled on an impressive training center in Toronto called BrainStation. If you visit their website, you'll see the UX Design Bootcamp with options from online to in-person locations—that is what she did. In January 2017, she found an Airbnb, booked her flight, and flew to Toronto for ten weeks of focused learning. The total cost of those ten weeks was less than half the cost of one semester of college.

It was intense, with thirty-plus hours a week focused exclusively on UX/UI through classroom learning, lab challenges, projects, one-on-one coaching, guest speakers, networking events, and more. Lauren loved it. As hoped, the more she learned, the more excited she became. During those ten weeks in Toronto, she decided her goal was to land a UX/UI Designer job.

After an intense eight months away—living two to three months each in Indonesia, San Francisco, and Toronto—Lauren decided to come home, catch her breath, and think through her next steps.

Okay, now you know what you want to try first as a job. You might be a UX/UI Designer for ten years or two years. There is no way to know, but this is how you want to start, so let's work toward that.

One of the hardest things to do is land your first job without experience. The college industry says a degree puts you ahead, but as you know, all a degree does is make you look like everyone else with a degree. So, the key now is to set yourself apart and motivate someone to give you a shot.

Start applying what you learned and building a portfolio to showcase your work. Continue your learning and amp up your networking. It might take a few weeks or several months to break through. Things might come easy, or you might get rejected many times. Some days, you'll feel energized and motivated; others, you'll feel desperate and frustrated.

Welcome to the real world.

She got a job as a server at Ted's Montana Grill (the referral letter mentioned earlier), which enabled her to save money, gain valuable experience engaging and talking with people, and have enough free time to do everything we discussed in the conversation above. About one year had passed since high school graduation, and Lauren's high school friends were back home after one year of college.

SUBSTANTIAL EARLY LEAD

Imagine you sit down with two nineteen-year-olds and learn what each of them did during the twelve months after high school graduation.

Teenager #1	Teenager #2
Lived in a dorm room and spent most of her time within a three-square-mile bubble.	Independently traveled the world and lived ten-plus weeks in three different countries.
Made good grades in general education classes in which she had little interest.	Self-directed and invested her learning, time, and money in pursuing her first full-time job.
Built friendships with people of the same age, stage of life, and (mostly) nationality.	Built friendships with people of vastly different ages, nationalities, and stages of life.
Had fun through the classic college experience of parties, football games, binge drinking, and intramural sports.	Had fun at a full-moon party in Bali, nightclubbing in Toronto, and crashing house parties in San Francisco.

Which nineteen-year-old would be more impressive to you? Which one would you want to learn more about? Which one would spark more questions? Then, imagine you're an employer asking yourself, "Which of these two people do I think is more adaptable, driven, and ready to add value to my organization right now?"

And that is the whole point of this book.

Why are parents convinced the key to success is for their teenager to do what everyone else does while wasting time and money pretending to grow up? Twelve months after high school, Lauren separated herself through unique experiences, focused learning, and soft-skill development. The gap expanded over the next three years because there were limitless options to advance, gain experience, and develop.

Looking back at Lauren's development, I recommend you help your teenager focus on six things at this stage.

1. Apprenticeship.
2. Rejection therapy.
3. Work for free.
4. Build a portfolio.
5. LinkedIn profile.
6. Shadow someone.

APPRENTICESHIP

An apprenticeship program enables attendees to develop soft skills, apply what they learn, and be guided to their first job. There are many programs across all types of careers. Some guarantee a job, others do not. Some require you to pay upfront, while others take a portion of your income once employed. Based on a few hours of research, you will likely find one that fits your teenager's goals and budget.

That's what Lauren did. At the same time her friends were returning to college for their second semester of sophomore year, an apprenticeship program enabled her to land her first full-time UX/UI Designer job with a start-up company based outside of Washington, DC.

But . . . what if your teenager either doesn't want to attend or cannot afford an apprenticeship program? Or, what if there isn't a good apprenticeship option in their field of interest? Then they focus their energy on developing transferable skills that, as mentioned earlier, are highly valued by employers and universally applicable to any role. These skills are critically important even if you have a college degree because (again, remember 0 for 300) today's hiring managers will not just hand you a job. You must make it happen.

REJECTION THERAPY

One of the best modules Lauren participated in during UnCollege was "Rejection Therapy," and I highly recommend you do your own version. In short, she was paired up with one other person and sent out on the streets of San Francisco, with each of them video recording the other's "rejection" attempts. They each had to walk up to a stranger and ask that person for or to do something. For example, Lauren asked strangers to

- let her listen to what they were listening to (share an earbud),
- get behind the counter and make a burrito, and
- race across the street when the "Walk Now" sign lit up.

Each request was made respectfully, of course; the result was that eight of her ten requests (eighty percent) resulted in a yes. Her partner achieved a similar result (as did everyone else in the cohort). She learned that one of life's most important keys is simply asking. If you don't ask, you'll never know what the outcome would have been. You'll usually find that, if you ask politely and respectfully, many people will say yes. It's a critical lesson for anyone to learn at any age.

WORK FOR FREE

Many people bristle at the idea of working for free—don't let your teenager be one of those people, especially when they're starting out and need to prove their value. Aggressively look for options to fulfill a need with the following type of outreach (use a combination of ChatGPT and Grammarly to quickly create and edit versions based on personal style, location, and role).

Example of outreach via email or LinkedIn

> Hello [Name],
>
> I am eager to embark on my career journey as a [insert profession] and recently noticed your need for assistance with [insert task]. Recognizing this as an opportunity to showcase my skills and dedication, I proactively addressed your request by completing [insert specific task or project]. You can view my progress [insert link] to see the results of my efforts thus far.
>
> Should you find my work compelling and wish to collaborate further, I am prepared to offer ten additional

hours of complimentary service. My goal is to ensure your complete satisfaction with the outcome. If I meet your requirements, I kindly request permission to incorporate this project into my professional portfolio.

If further refinement or additional tasks are necessary beyond the initial ten hours, I am open to a mutually agreeable hourly rate for continued collaboration. I am committed to delivering high-quality results that align with your objectives.

This pitch is a great way to start your career, especially if you're nineteen years old, already earning income as a restaurant server, and have plenty of free time with a low cost of living.

BUILD A PORTFOLIO

No matter the work, always showcase it. The presentation will vary based on the nature of the work, but you will find lots of free online courses, videos, and best practices. If this isn't a strength, offer to barter with a web designer. You can provide something of equal value in exchange for help building a portfolio or website. This is how you get ahead in today's economy and job market.

You can view Lauren's portfolio at her personal website (http://www.lpmarlowe.com), which has numerous examples of her work, including a website she offered to build for free early on.

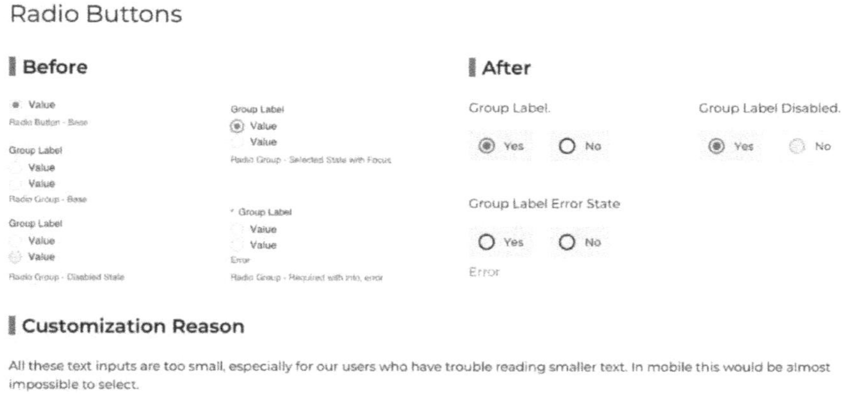

Figure 33. One of many samples from Lauren's online portfolio, which she started in 2019.

LINKEDIN PROFILE

A LinkedIn profile is a must to start a career and build a network. Think of it as an online résumé, and again, many free resources are available to learn how to create a great profile. Don't overinvest, however, as most people will not read every detail. Keep it crisp, accurate, and professional—no spelling or grammar errors, and no fluff.

After crafting a profile, you use LinkedIn to search for and connect with professionals in any field who can offer career insights, introductions to relevant networks, referral opportunities, and much more. As you'll see on Lauren's profile (https://www.linkedin.com/in/laurenmarlowe/), she has over four hundred connections with people of all ages and from all industries, demographics, and global locations. People can network on LinkedIn by making a regular connection request or sending a direct message via its premium InMail service. An example of this "cold" contact request type is provided below.

Example of outreach via email or LinkedIn

> Hello [Name],
>
> I'm eager to kickstart my journey in the [insert profession] field. I came across your profile on LinkedIn and was impressed by your [insert number] years of experience in this industry. I'm intrigued by your career trajectory and would like to spend 30 minutes with you to gain insights into how you navigated it.
>
> As a token of appreciation for your time, I'd like to offer you a small gesture of gratitude. I'm happy to 1) assist with some "grunt" work at no cost, 2) treat you to coffee if you're local, or 3) send you a $20 Amazon gift card.
>
> Thank you for considering my request, and I look forward to connecting with you soon.
>
> Best regards,
>
> [Your Name]

If you connect with someone you've met, you can browse that person's LinkedIn network and find connections in the same field of interest.

Example of outreach via email or LinkedIn

> Hello [Name],
>
> As we briefly touched upon last week, I'm embarking on a new chapter in my career journey, aiming to dive into the world of [insert profession]. Upon exploring your LinkedIn profile, I couldn't help but notice your connections with [Name 1] and [Name 2], both impressive individuals in the field I aspire to enter. Would you be open to facilitating introductions?
>
> If so, I will ghostwrite an email to request 30 minutes to delve into their career trajectories—how they embarked on their journeys and navigated their way to success. In appreciation for their time and insights, I will offer to 1) assist with two hours of "grunt" work free of charge, 2) treat them to a coffee meeting if they're local, or 3) send a $20 Amazon gift card.
>
> I appreciate your assistance in making these connections and will happily reciprocate. Thank you for considering my request, and I look forward to your response.
>
> Warm regards,
>
> [Your Name]

LinkedIn is a fantastic way to research and find professionals, each potentially willing to lend a helping hand (always offer to return the favor).

SHADOW SOMEONE

Once you build connections in your field of interest, try to "shadow" someone in your desired role, getting a firsthand look at the day-to-day work. For example, someone interested in interior design would reach out to people as explained above. Then, request such an opportunity by demonstrating professionalism, politeness, and helpfulness.

Example of outreach via email or LinkedIn

[Recipient's Name],

I wanted to express my heartfelt gratitude for your support and guidance throughout my exploration of interior design. The deeper I delve into this field, the more my passion ignites. Yet, one crucial aspect I lack is real-world experience—seeing the ins and outs of what it truly means to be an interior designer.

Can you grant me the opportunity to shadow you for two to three days? I understand the importance of your time and expertise and want to offer value in return. Given our previous conversations, offering to babysit your kids for a few days or evenings, free of charge, could be a meaningful gesture of gratitude.

If you're open to me riding shotgun with you, I'm eager to hear your thoughts on how I can seamlessly integrate into your workflow with minimal disruption. Your insight and mentorship would be invaluable to me, and I appreciate any opportunity to learn from you firsthand.

Thank you for considering my request.

Warm regards,

[Your Name]

Adjust what you offer in return accordingly—make it something you know will be helpful to the person being asked. During the shadow, pay attention to all elements of the job because, inevitably, the most enjoyable parts only represent a percentage of what is done. Sometimes the percentage is high, which is great, but sometimes it's much lower—this is likely a red flag. If you commit to starting a career, you want to do so with eyes wide open.

Try before you buy

THRIVING

When teenagers succumb to pressure to decide what they want to "be" without understanding the day-to-day job in the real world, they're flying blind. I'll always believe it's far better to complete rejection therapy, lose your fear of asking, start networking, and take some time to try before you buy.

When her high school peers were starting their junior year of college, still two years and *lots* of money away from trying to find their first job, Lauren had been employed full-time at a tech start-up and financially independent for six months. She commuted to work daily, hit the gym in the evenings, explored Washington, DC, and built new friendships. To accelerate her career and secure her dream job, she had to master creating unique value for others.

CHAPTER 30

Create Unique Value for Others

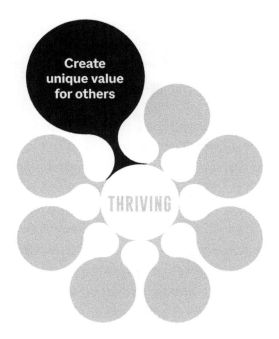

For the first 175 years after the Industrial Revolution, the world and its "jobs" evolved slowly. What made sense for one generation generally made sense for the next generation, and that's what school was designed for. But then everything changed. For our final Seth Godin quote:[5]

---

5 Seth Godin, *Stop Stealing Dreams* (2014), https://seths.blog/wp-content/uploads/2014/09/stop-stealing-dreams-print.pdf.

One of the factors that made hard labor palatable was that the economy didn't offer a lot of choices. If you worked in Lackawanna, you probably worked a farm or steel mill. It's not like you spent a great deal of time wondering about what you might be doing instead.

Today, choices are everywhere. Which means that not only do we have to wrestle with insufficiency (of respect, of compensation, of reliable work), but we also have to take responsibility for our freedom. The freedom to choose something better and, even more important, the freedom to do work that matters.

The traditional approach of picking and staying in a job for decades is now irrelevant. There is no longer any reason for someone to limit themselves in that way, because "choices are everywhere." You can wish it wasn't so, lament how things are, or hope things return to how they used to be, but that only makes you a relic. In today's world, achieving and maintaining financial success while taking responsibility for your freedom to do work that matters comes down to the ability to continuously evolve such that you uniquely create value for others. The simplest way to achieve that is to become the kind of person others value. How do you do that?

Stop and think about two or three awe-inspiring people you know. Not athletes or entertainers, but people you interact with daily who've got it going on. People you look up to or hope to one day be more like. As you do so, what traits come to mind? For me, it is traits like these:

- Exudes calm, unshakable self-confidence.
- Smart, but much more in a wise kind of way versus spouting a bunch of facts.
- Reads a room, picks their spots, and blends into almost any conversation.
- Active listener who makes others feel valued and heard.

- Completely comfortable in their own skin; the opposite of hypersensitive.
- Almost always contributes a positive attitude and energy but doesn't overdo it.
- Witty or, at minimum, a good sense of humor.
- Reliable, solid, stable; the opposite of frantic.

Your traits might differ, but we all know an impressive person when we meet one, and when you do, you want to find ways to be around and learn from them. If you need something important done, you hope they will do it for you (or help you do it). You will repeatedly be given opportunities to create value when you're impressive to others. And that is the guidance you want to give your teenager.

Because you're not wasting time pursuing a credential, you get to invest time learning how to become valuable to others. The more valuable you become, the more opportunities you will gain access to. Becoming valuable is easier than it might seem. It's common sense.

Let's document what we mutually agree to be the traits and characteristics of the most impressive people we know and interact with. The kind of people you're sure must be valuable to others. It will likely feel unattainable as we build our list, especially at a young age. However, always remember that being impressive and standing out is primarily about exceeding people's expectations for "someone like you."

When you venture into the real world at eighteen or nineteen and start your first job, no one expects much of you. So, your secret weapon is to focus your time and energy on developing a few of the traits on our list that are rarely displayed by young adults (most of whom are busy memorizing information and studying for tests).

Doing so will lead to value creation and lift you above the fray.

FIVE KEY ATTRIBUTES TO EXUDE

While you and your teenager should create your own list of traits, I will share what I believe to be the five most important attributes for your teenager to develop and have in their tool kit when they venture into the real world. If they consistently demonstrate these attributes, they will exceed expectations of "someone like you" and gain access to opportunities early on.

First, **have a great attitude**. Be a positive, kind, and low-maintenance individual. Early in your career, refrain from making demands, and if you do, be highly selective. Look people in the eye and have a confident handshake. You want everyone interacting with you to conclude, "I am impressed by your attitude."

Second, **fit in**. I will be blunt—you haven't earned the right to influence or change the culture in your workplace. If you find it toxic, get out; otherwise, fit in. As you do, be observant; watch what successful people do and act like them. You want everyone interacting with you to conclude, "I love how easily you fit right in and do things the way we want them done around here."

Third, **be reliable**. Always be on time or, better yet, early. When you commit to something, do it, period. Do not make excuses. Focus on working hard (you can focus on working smart later). You want everyone interacting with you to conclude, "I love how you get things done, no matter what is asked."

Fourth, **exhibit curiosity**. Take the time to understand why the organization exists and its mission statement about what it does and how it does it. Locate intelligent people and ask them for a quick chat to help you do so. Come to those conversations with thoughtful questions, take notes, and follow up to confirm you "got it right." You want everyone interacting with you to conclude, "I am so impressed by your dedication to what we're most trying to achieve as an organization."

Fifth, **be solution-oriented**. As you learn what the organization is trying to achieve, rather than point out problems or things you think can be done better, selectively pick a problem and share a potential solution. Instead of saying, "We should ___," approach your manager and say, "I noticed ___ and built ___ as a potentially better way. Do you think I should keep going on this?" You want everyone interacting with you to conclude, "I appreciate how you proactively strive to solve problems—keep it up."

Opportunities will come your teenager's way if they consistently do these five things at the start of their career. As they do, with each opportunity, there are three core ways to accelerate their development and ability to create unique value for others consistently.

DO NOT MAKE ASSUMPTIONS

With experience, you will learn how to work smarter and make the correct assumptions. However, you must refrain from assuming anything, and validate everything early on. Even if the opportunity is straightforward, such as, "Deliver this package to this important customer by 2:00 p.m. latest," validate everything. To the person giving you the opportunity or task, ask good questions:

- I don't want to take any chances—can I deliver the package early? If so, how early?
- Do I need to deliver it to a specific individual? Do I deliver it to a front desk or an assistant?
- If I cannot locate the right person or location for any reason, who do I contact?
- Etc.

You don't want to be annoying and ask an avalanche of questions, so take some time to jot down only those necessary to ensure you know *exactly* how to deliver the package. For a more "advanced" opportunity, the same approach applies. For example, if given the responsibility to "evaluate this data and find out why we're not profitable on this product," ask questions such as:

- What profit margin was this product designed to achieve versus what profit margin is currently being achieved?

- Most products have a ramp time to profitability—when was this product supposed to achieve the desired profit margin?
- Do we sell similar products with similar profit margin goals? If so, how successful are those products, and can I access that data?
- Etc.

The more advanced the opportunity, the more advanced the questions. If you're unsure what to ask or if an opportunity is beyond your current capabilities, it's perfectly okay to (1) ask for help or (2) decline and suggest another, more qualified person to take it on.

CLARIFY EXPECTATIONS

Once (or perhaps before) you agree to take on an opportunity, understand exactly what is expected of you. In the "deliver a package by 2:00 p.m." scenario above, the expectation is clear, but for a more advanced opportunity, you should clarify things like:
- When do you need this assessment to be completed?
- Is it your expectation that I do this assessment independently, or can I request help from ____ or ____ as needed?
- In what format do you need my assessment delivered (slides, a document, a verbal presentation, a combination . . .)?
- If I get a few hours into this and get stuck, is it okay to come back to you and ask for help?
- Etc.

Seasoned professionals can renegotiate or push back on expectations. When starting out, however, strive to fully understand what is expected and then find a way to exceed expectations.

EXCEED EXPECTATIONS

Always find ways to exceed the expectations others have for you and/or the opportunity given to you. Let's go back to the "deliver this package" opportunity. Once you've ensured a thorough understanding of expectations and eliminated any assumptions, find a way to exceed those expectations. For example:

- If the customer has an assistant, contact that person and let them know you're bringing a package today.
- Ask what the customer loves to eat for lunch when ordering out and what time is best for you to have it there, and ask the assistant what they'd like for lunch.
- Leave early, order ahead, pick up the food, and deliver it (and the package) at the agreed-upon time.

When you get back to work, let whoever gave you this opportunity know you delivered the package early and decided to take lunch to the customer and their assistant as a thank you for being one of your best customers. You will likely be told, "Wow, that is amazing; thank you for going above and beyond. Send me a receipt so I can reimburse you for the lunch."

Even with the most straightforward opportunity, you can always find a way to deliver unique value (something other people don't think to do). With the more advanced "research this data" opportunity, perhaps do something like this:

- If you agree to complete your assessment in five days, on day two, deliver an organized "opening statement" of your findings so far and ask for feedback.
- As you do your data analysis, locate a similar type of product— either internally or from a competitor—and research it.
- If you were asked to deliver a simple write-up in a Word document, do that *and* create a simple spreadsheet with a few charts, and deliver your assessment in a visual presentation tool such as PowerPoint, Keynote, Canva, or Prezi (you can learn any of them for free). Keep it crisp; less is more.
- Deliver your assessment—for two products, not just one—at least one day early.

To summarize, focus on mastering the five key attributes listed above, do not make assumptions, clarify what is expected of you, and find ways to exceed those expectations. This is how Lauren started her career and landed her dream job after three years. It had nothing to do with a GPA or credentials.

LAND AND EXPAND

In addition to what I just outlined, four aspects of a young adult's mindset lead to consistent growth, fulfillment, and prosperity in today's dynamic world.

First, lean into change. I emphasize embracing uncertainty and rethinking risk because today's economy and job market demand it. If you're scared of change and expect to pick a career/get a job/keep a job, you're likely in for a rude awakening (remember 0 for 300?). Instead, appreciate that, unlike previous generations, you are not stuck doing the same job for decades. Early in her career, Lauren was never afraid to pivot. She started creating a real estate–focused product at a start-up tech company, then shifted to a large financial services company where she designed consumer-facing applications, and then felt ready to pursue her "dream job."

Second, once you gain enough experience to pursue your "dream" job (please do so after finding your game and doing a good bit of try before you buy), specifically define what you want/need/expect at that point in your life so that you will feel excited and motivated when you wake up each morning. That is what work should feel like (not chasing titles and money).

Lauren defined her dream job as having these features:
- Large, multinational organization (vertical and horizontal opportunities).
- Travel-related industry (travel perks are a huge upside for her lifestyle).
- Work-from-anywhere policy (post-COVID, sought flexibility).
- Strong benefits, especially healthcare (cancer survivor).
- Great culture: inclusive, diverse.

- Options for B2B (business-to-business) and B2C (business-to-consumer) design.
- Competitive compensation (salary + benefits + bonus + potential equity).

As previously outlined, she landed this dream job through a recruiter connecting her to a hiring manager at a Fortune 200 global airline company. She bypassed the online filtering system, presented a highly polished portfolio, nailed every interview, and left no doubt she was the best candidate. That is how you kick ass in today's world: not by getting an outdated credential everyone else has, applying online, and hoping to be noticed.

Third, even if you land your dream job within a high-income and apparently stable field, you must continuously evolve and deliver value. Pay attention to changes and advancements in your field (Lauren is aggressively learning about AI on her own). Constantly develop hard and soft skills. Proactively seek and pounce on opportunities to deliver value. Don't be afraid to ask for feedback and, once received, apply it.

Last, you will accelerate your access to value-creation opportunities by building high-trust relationships with people who will think about you when they encounter compelling situations. This starts slowly when you're young and builds over time. Lauren purposefully builds relationships with sharp, emotionally intelligent, and driven people through whom many opportunities for mutual value creation might present themselves.

This mindset is why a college degree is almost always unnecessary to start and advance within virtually any career you choose. Without ever spending a minute in a college classroom, Lauren is now six years into a high-paying, challenging, and (for her) incredibly fulfilling career.

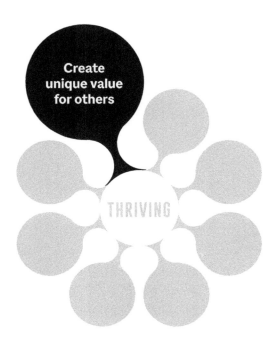

To fully recap, between the ages of eighteen and twenty-three while her high school peers were on a college campus, Lauren

- taught English to young kids in a remote village in Bali, Indonesia;
- lived (three-plus months each) in San Francisco, Toronto, and Washington, DC;
- taught herself everything from German and Spanish ("good enough to get by"), to how to save and invest money, to how to interview and to how to negotiate a raise;
- traveled to and spent several weeks in Europe (multiple countries) and Mexico;
- built friendships with people from all over the world, several of whom she stays in touch with, travels with, hosts, and is hosted by;
- identified a high-paying, in-demand career (UX/UI) that fit her skill set and landed a job;
- faced and defeated stage 3 cancer;
- became financially independent at the age of twenty and has lived on her own since;

- transitioned to her second job and increased her income to a level higher than the average Harvard graduate earns in their first year; and
- landed her dream job, moved to her dream city (San Diego), and established her dream lifestyle (heavy travel).

That is quite a five-year experience. Was it a better or worse experience compared to the traditional path and college? I don't know, but who cares? It was her experience, and she enjoyed most of it. She's a thriving young adult who believes her journey made her who she is today.

Before you sit down with your teenager to work on everything in the last three chapters, I encourage you to do a quick role-play in your mind. You have important things you need someone to do and will pay a handsome salary. Imagine you hire that person and, from day one, they

- display a great attitude— they're upbeat and say "no problem" when asked to do something;
- fit right into your day-to-day operating mode, bring no drama, and make no demands;
- show up early or, worst case, on time and deliver what is asked with no complaints;
- demonstrate unwavering curiosity about what you need most and how to create value; and
- proactively attempt to solve problems or challenges without being asked.

Can you picture this person in your mind? How do you feel about them? When you consider the importance of what you need, how valuable is this person to you? Exactly. Now, stop telling your teenager to study for their biology test, and instead, help them become that person you imagined.

Figure 34. Lauren in Colombia, South America.

Figure 35. Lauren doing "below the wing" research for her UX/UI job at a global airline.

Figure 36. Lauren in Lake Tahoe, Nevada.

Figure 37. Lauren in Lisbon, Portugal.

FAQS I HEAR OR CAN PREDICT

Isn't a sample size of one too small to draw conclusions?

While I detailed Lauren's journey, there are countless others. My best friend dropped out of college after two years and has held C-level executive positions for the last fifteen years. There are millions of companies desperately seeking talent. Credentials are optional.

Isn't it possible Lauren is just an outlier?

While I love her endlessly, and she's intelligent and adventurous, Lauren isn't some prodigy or outlier. She prepared herself to be different.

She didn't wallow in the comfort of certainty, follow the crowd, or feel scared by the challenge of designing her own "once-in-a-lifetime experience." Instead, she thought big, became excited by uncertainty, and placed no limits on what she could choose to do. While other teenagers devoted hours to straight As, SAT prep, and filling out college applications, she used that time to explore her strengths, research how to travel safely, and undertake self-development activities. Once she landed her first job, she focused on value creation, displaying a great attitude and keeping her portfolio current. None of that requires prodigious talent.

Right, but what do I do if my teenager doesn't have the "long-term vision" Lauren did?

Oh gosh, no—Lauren didn't have a grand, long-term vision. After graduating high school, Lauren only knew what she would try first—UnCollege. It was a six-month program she believed would help her start exploring. That was it.

She didn't know what type of job she wanted to pursue initially. She was struggling with self-identity. Her confidence was only starting to build and often waned. She was more awkward than polished around most people. While she prepared herself to be different, she figured she would start with UnCollege and then take it from there.

Similar to her sister's experience, one thing led to another.

What if my teenager really wants to go to college?

Did you and your teenager exhaustively evaluate all options post–high school and choose college as the clear "winner?" Does your teenager clearly understand the hard, soft, and opportunity costs of college? Suppose your teenager is determined to enter a career that requires a certification or degree (such as a surgeon or CPA). Have they done exhaustive research to fully "feel" what it's like to do that job? Have you explained the potential downside of an "all eggs in one basket" approach?

If the answer to those questions is a resounding "yes," I applaud the decision to attend college.

Does Lauren have any concerns that she'll hit a ceiling?

She has zero concerns. Six years into her career, she's observed hundreds of situations in which people are assessed, promoted, fired, rewarded, ignored, and guided. She's never—not once—heard someone say, "If only so and so had a college degree," or similar. She has yet to encounter a single person—not one—who brought up her lack of a college degree. No one cares. And if someone eventually does care, she will leave and work with and for the tens of millions of people who do not care about something so shallow and meaningless.

Lauren's journey was highly adventurous; what if my teenager is far more conservative?

I encourage you to think through three things.

First, get to the root cause of their conservatism. School uses fear to drive conformity. Make sure the conservative nature isn't a by-product of conforming. If it is, help them build a new mindset.

Second, if they're genuinely conservative, suggest a journey more like Brooke's. She didn't travel the world or attend boot camps. She gradually found herself while living fifteen minutes from her parents. Suggest a remote development program, like Praxis, that they can participate in while still starting to work. There are lots of options.

Last, do not assume your teenager is incapable of things, because they will assume you're right. If you do not introduce and encourage them to consider new things, they will default to what everyone else does. And if you tell them the world is a dangerous place and it's best to stay in their bubble, they will be scared to take a risk.

As I said earlier, please don't allow a lazy mindset of doing what everyone else does because it's convenient or safe. Be better than that. Be more interesting than that.

Conclusion

Until now, your teenager has been told academic excellence and credentials are critical for their future financial stability and happiness. The best way to learn is by receiving instruction in a fixed way or system. Following the rules and doing what others tell you is the best way to prepare for early adulthood. Breaking the rules, or even worse, making your own rules, is dangerous. College is the only way to attain the required credentials to be eligible for the best jobs and careers.

Based on what they're told, they put their head down, suppress their hopes and dreams, and comply because there are tasks to complete, tests to ace, grades to attain, applications to fill out, and a flawless "permanent record" to compile.

But no more.

With you as their guide, your teenager can step off the linear, formulaic, and unnecessary path and design their unique journey. If I could sit down face-to-face with your potentially skeptical and self-conscious teenager today, I would tell them:

You can believe what you see on TV and social media and what you hear from supposed experts about what is best for you as an individual. You can believe that a one-size-fits-all education system is the best way to learn and develop your mind. You can think there are lots of hard-and-fast rules in the real world and that you, as an individual, must follow them.

You can continue the pattern of high stress, anxiety, and worry as you look ahead to your future. And you can believe that investing four years of your life at an almost incalculable cost is table stakes for everyone.

You can choose to believe all those things with no questions asked and no curiosity. You can do what everyone else does because it feels safe and easy, and hope it works out.

Or, with guidance from your parent(s), you can take control of what you learn, your expectations, and how you confidently step out into a real world that's not nearly as scary as you are led to believe.

Doing so does not mean everything will be easy, that bad things will not happen, or you will not face adversity. As the saying goes, nothing worth having comes easy. It means you will build the necessary mindset to take on hard things, deal with adversity, and achieve your version of success and happiness (which will constantly change).

I hope you're not just ready but bursting at the seams with excitement to escape the pressure of other people's expectations and start to enjoy the freedom and self-confidence gained when you do (with guidance and mentoring) what you want to do.

I will close with this.

If you are convinced credentials will matter, set the pursuit aside for now and come back to it only after your teenager develops a growth mindset, becomes adept at self-directed learning and expectation-setting, builds their emotional intelligence, starts doing things that make them feel accomplished, steps out into the real world, learns the cost of things, finds their game, tries before they buy, and dabbles with creating unique value for others. All those things can easily be accomplished during their teenage years if they're not investing countless hours pursuing grades and high achievement. If you both remain convinced a credential is necessary after your teenager does these things, *then* go get it.

Remember that many will insist you're making a colossal mistake by veering off course. Your teenager might even be called to the principal's office at a public high school with over 1,500 students and be told, "You have so much potential, and you'll never reach it if you don't go to college. Don't limit yourself. Please change your mind, commit to what we know is required, and focus on college."

When Lauren told me she heard that from her school principal, I couldn't help but chuckle (fun word; we should say it more often). By then, she was confident, prepared, and excited about her first step after high school. She's proven that principal wrong many times over.

Now it's time for your teenager to do the same thing. Go make it happen.

About the Author

Seth Marlowe is a rookie author who firmly believes in shaking things up regarding the well-trodden path society expects teenagers to follow. A Southern boy through and through, he was born in Columbus, Georgia, and grew up in Charlotte, North Carolina, where he and his wife, Donna, currently reside. Together, they had the joy of raising two wonderful daughters—Lauren, now twenty-six, and Brooke, now twenty-three.

Over the past two decades, those who've shared quality time with Seth know his enthusiasm for challenging the traditional narrative surrounding academic excellence and predefined life paths for teenagers. This passion is laid bare in his debut book, *Pathbreaker Parenting*, where he dismantles conventional notions and provides profound insights, sparking fresh, empowering conversations between parents and teens.

Seth built a successful thirty-year career in the business world through a combination of roles in sales, customer success, and mid-level management, and as a senior executive. He volunteered hundreds of hours to facilitate leadership training for rising juniors and seniors in high school, which serves as the heartbeat of this book. Outside of his wordsmith adventures and parenting crusades, you'll find Seth trying (and usually failing) to play tennis, cheering on his hometown sports teams through thick and (mostly) thin, savoring Donna's exquisite culinary creations, delving into a stack of nonfiction books, and going the extra mile (or ten) to pick the brains of teenagers and young adults.

Visit his website at pathbreakerparenting.com to learn more about his background and sign up for emails.

If you have questions about *Pathbreaker Parenting*
or want to discuss partnership opportunities,
please email me at

SETH@PATHBREAKERPARENTING.COM

Podcast and Blog:

PATHBREAKERPARENTING.COM

Connect with Me:

PATHBREAKER-PARENTING

PATHBREAKERPARENTING

Beth,

While we've not met in person,
I'm glad I've gotten to know
you a bit. Thank you for
the support and encouragement
these last few years. I hope
you enjoy the read!

Sam

Printed in the USA
CPSIA information can be obtained
at www.ICGtesting.com
CBHW052223030624
9339CB00009B/14